What they're saying about
The Dragon Complex

"Sporadic icidents of rage are all too common in our society today. This book examines one aspect of this dysfunctional mentality and shows ways that we can correct the problem."

—Edith Clark
Retired University Professor

"It is impossible to be fully productive in an environment in which psychological abuse, however hidden, is present. Dragons are very clever at masking their activities. As a leader in the workplace, the CEO has the responsibility of addressing and solving the problem."

—Carl Heintz
Business Owner

"Vanquish the Dragon and restore prosperity to the village! This book shows how the workplace community can identify its hidden monsters, smoke them out, and end their terrorizing reign."

—Debra Karr, Ph.D.

"Everyone has known a Dragon: whether it's on the playground, at home, or in the workplace. Finally a book reveals the destructive relationship between power and abuse that appears in a dysfunctional workplace. The authors provide ways to identify and halt the effects of this psychological warfare."

—JoAnn Fister
Counselor

The Dragon Complex:

Strategies for Identifying and Conquering Workplace Abuse

By

Winnifred Taylor, Ph.D.

Patrick C. Dorin, Ph.D.

John Taylor, Ph.D.

PUBLISHER'S NOTE

This publication is designed to provide accurate and authoritative information in regard to the subject matter covered. It is sold with the understanding that the authors and the publisher are not engaged in rendering legal, medical, psychological, or other professional service. If legal, psychological, or other expert assistance is required, the service of a competent professional person should be sought.

Cypress Publishing Group, Inc.

1835 Roe # 187
Leawood, KS 66211
www.cypresspublishing.com

Library of Congress Cataloging-in-Publication Data

Dorin, Patrick C., John Taylor, Winnifred Taylor
The Dragon Complex / by Dorin et al.
Includes glossary, bibliography
p. cm.
ISBN: 0-89447-327-1
1. Psychology – Workplace. 2. Business – Employee Relations. I. Title.

Cover art by Bob Bliss
Edited by Amanda Sanders

Printed in the United States of America

10 9 8 7 6 5 4 3 2 1

Table Of Contents

Acknowledgments

Introduction 1

Step I Recognize the Mystification
Chapter 1 Victimization by Mystification 7
Chapter 2 What You Need to Know to Get Started 23

Step II Unmask the Dragon
Chapter 3 Dragon Tracking 29
Chapter 4 Power Games Dragons Play 53

Step III Honor Your Anger
Chapter 5 Trust Your Anger Alarm 67
Chapter 6 Deal with Depression 83
Chapter 7 Handling Stress 91

Step IV Disarm the Dragons
Chapter 8 Hang on to Your Beliefs 103
Chapter 9 Dragon Fire Extinguishers 115
Chapter 10 Subtle Abuse 137
Chapter 11 Deliberate Abuse 155

Step V Take Action
Chapter 12 Look at All the Options 171
Chapter 13 Do It! 201

Epilogue: 219
A Word to the Organization
Advice for the Therapist
A Note to the EAP Counselor

Appendix I: A Postscript for the Reader 229

Appendix II: Comparative Abuse 237

Bibliography 241

Glossary 243

Acknowledgments

The authors would like to thank the following people for their thoughts, insights, suggestions, proofreading, recommendations, and patience: Karen M. Dorin, Timothy Taylor, Ph.D., Toby Marcovich, Sandra Wright, Charles Jensen, Dana Parask, Joy Johnson, Michael Musgrave, and Michael Burlaga.

Thanks to Kelly Burger and Ginny Garner-Gerhardt of CASDA (The Center Against Sexual and Domestic Abuse, Superior, Wisconsin) who assisted us in locating materials containing Biderman's Chart of Coercion.

We wish to thank Carl Heintz and Amanda Sanders of Cypress Publishing Group, Inc., who provided crucial editorial and layout work for the production of this book.

A special note of thanks to all the individuals, organization, and companies who were brave enough to share their stories and concerns so that others can understand that a person is not alone in the trials of working in an abusive and dysfunctional environment. Many people over the past ten years and longer have discussed their circumstances and working environments on the condition of confidentiality. Therefore, the names of the individuals and organizations have been changed to protect their confidentiality. Should any names of individuals or organizations reflect real circumstances with which the reader may be familiar, it is purely coincidental.

We wish to to thank the following publishing companies for their kind assistance and permission to quote materials from their publications: Scott Plikerd, McGraw-Hill Education; Jonathan Campbell, John Wiley & Sons; Ronald E. McMullen, American Psychiatric Publishing; Michael Graves, Random House; Amnesty International; and William Morrow & Company.

Thank you, each and every one, for your kind assistance obtaining the information and materials used in this book.

Introduction

Marilyn worked for a large defense contractor. She had to work long hours and take work home evenings and weekends to appease her boss, who claimed that her work was consistently below par. She eventually suffered a breakdown and was promptly replaced.

Josh works as an accountant for a large insurance company. He is threatened with losing his job if he will not help his supervisor "adjust the books" to reflect a profit by inflating revenues. He knows his actions are wrong and could result in deceiving shareholders and officers, but he fears he could be fired and blacklisted from the industry if he doesn't go along.

Rick supervises a production line. His boss insists that Rick hire "phantom workers" and give their paychecks to him. Rick initially refused to do so but was told that he would be fired if he refused. After he reluctantly complied one time, he was told that he must continue, or he will be held responsible for the theft and sent to jail.

Jenny is often asked to cover for her boss when he takes the afternoon off to play golf. She is instructed to lie to anyone who calls. She has intense loyalty to her boss, whom she fears at the same time because she has seen his fits of rage and abusive treatment of those who cross his path.

These people have been the victims of Dragons, those within the workplace in a position of power who abuse, manipulate, and often destroy their targets in a vicious ploy for personal power. Often they use clever psychological manipulation, and they are usually masters of camouflage and deception. Employees, management, or human resources personnel may not even be aware that the company has Dragons in its midst until the toll of low productivity, broken careers, and lost opportunities becomes overwhelming. By that time, the Dragon has usually moved on.

Who are these Dragons, and where do they come from?

Have you ever wondered what happened to those playground bullies you knew in grade school? According to recent research, a fourth of them end up in prison as adults. What happens to the rest? A small percentage outgrow their bully personalities and go on to live normal lives. The rest end up in the workforce. There, the bullying personality matures and exhibits itself in many subtle and not-so-subtle ways. As they grow up, bullies learn how to abuse people without hitting them; they learn how to use psychology to harass and demean their targets. It's the same story as in third grade: the bully usurps power and uses it to dominate the playground or classroom. Adult bullies are often clever manipulators and skilled perpetrators of crowd control. They intimidate others into following them, they instill fear, and they are often brilliant at succeeding through psychological manipulation.

This book describes the pathology underlying the power and control needs of abusive individuals, who often become managers or supervisors. We choose to call these people "Dragons." Dragons enjoy undermining the careers of any employees who are perceived as threats and/or will not be a part of inappropriate activities. Employees may be targeted because of their high knowledge levels; positive working relationships with staff, customers and clients; progressive suggestions; questioning of new or unspoken business practices; or pointing out potential problems.

Abusive bosses are cunning enough to know that they can't just fire productive people. It would make the abusive bosses look foolish. Therefore, they have a field day creating a case for dismissal under the guise that it is "good for the company." The confused victims, blaming job stress, often accept the guilt for their perceived and/or trumped-up "failures" without question, while the abuser feels victorious.

Dragons, because of fear and insecurities, believe they must be in control of everyone in their area. If any individual is perceived to be a possible threat to the Dragon, that individual must be driven out! Therefore, these quality people must be removed regardless of the short- or long-term damage done to the organization. This is done to alleviate the Dragon's own paranoia, lack of knowledge about the organization, or inability to work with people.

Dragons are afraid to surround themselves with excellence. They hire only those people who are perceived to be less intelligent, which creates a "dumbing-down" of the organization. Dragons must also form protective circles of people, Doorkeepers, in order to maintain and continually increase their power and control. If an individual is perceived as a possible supporter, that person is subjected to a "test" by the Dragon. Such tests come in a variety of forms, such as getting the individual to be a part of dishonest or other inappropriate activities or demonstrating a willingness to follow along and destroy another employee. If the selected person does not pass the "test" or fits one of the high-quality categories listed above, the newly designated victim must be targeted for both destruction and constructive dismissal. Considering Dragon insecurities, dismissal from the organization is often not enough for a Dragon. The victim's career must also be destroyed.

This dismissal process is shrouded with mystification that includes subtle and long-term mind games that proceed until the victim is ready to snap. It is a strategy designed to set people up for failure over a period of time – to create a solid basis for dismissal with the appearance that it is the target's own fault!

Dragons, because of their power and control needs, always have people who are targeted for destruction. It can be a single individual or many on an unwritten list. Furthermore, Dragons do not simply target individuals for destruction. Their strategies include pitting individuals, as well as entire departments, against each other, all the while using "buzz" words like cooperation and team approaches. When departments are pitted against each other, the abusive boss feels a sense of safety because there is no unity, and thus no power, among the various groups. It is all part of the mystification process.

We wrote this book because we found many people who felt frustrated and angry with their work environment but did not fully comprehend what was happening. Our clients often expressed the situation as "job stress," but it is not job stress! Targeted individuals often suffer serious health problems. One person, who was subtly driven out of his middle-management marketing position, reported that what happened was "good for the company." Since he was in denial and did not have a working plan, his depression deepened after his dismissal, and he suffered a stroke. The company subsequently lost a substantial percentage of business in the manager's area with the explanation being that it was a "correction in the market place."

Denial of these tactics is widespread in the organizations that suffer from Dragons, as well as in our communities. It's the same old story, the same one you may have heard on the playground when bullying behavior was ignored or excused. This denial is so ingrained that a new level of understanding, or wake-up call, is desperately needed for:

- Targets of Dragon bosses, now or in the past
- Employees who are not yet targets but are at risk
- Managers, executives, and supervisors
- Families and friends of targets
- People in abusive relationships
- Psychologists, counselors, and other human services personnel
- Health professionals
- Union officials and other employee representatives
- Professional management consulting firms
- Schools of Business
- Legal firms

Patrick C. Dorin, Ph.D.

Winnifred F. Taylor, Ph.D.

John F. Taylor, Ph.D.

Step I
Recognize the Mystification

Step I shows you what you need to know about the mystique of dealing with a Dragon and how to begin doing something about it. Chapter 1 and Chapter 2 detail **Victimization by Mystification** and **What You Need to Know to Get Started**.

6 The Dragon Complex

Chapter 1

Victimization by Mystification

An excellent and highly skilled person with positive working relationships, who is perceived by a Dragon boss as a potential threat because of that knowledge and skill level, cannot simply be fired. A Dragon boss, because of power/control needs and fear, will desperately want to get rid of the person and will therefore carry out the *victimization through mystification process* with a variety of sneaky stages.

The targeted victim must not know what is really happening or comprehend that the ultimate goal of the boss is constructive dismissal. If the targeted employee did understand, or eventually begins to figure out the mystification process as well as the ultimate goal, it could mean resistance, and a Dragon boss cannot handle such resistance. The following is an example of a research person who had a strong knowledge of the company and had very positive working relationships but also had the misfortune of getting a new Dragon boss.

> Jerry had worked in a production/marketing research position for the B Company for 14 years. It was an unusual job in industry, because all too often, there is no real connection between marketing and production. Jerry reported to a vice president for twelve of these years, until a new president began a restructuring program. Jerry's vice president retired and was replaced by a person from one of B's competitors, Joe.
>
> At first, things seemed to go well, but within three months of Joe's arrival, a negative atmosphere was becoming more prevalent. Furthermore, the department meetings were filled with one-way dialogues on the need for change and how restructuring was going to make the company more profitable. However, customer needs and employee morale were never addressed in connection with

the promotion for change. In fact, specific change strategies were never even mentioned in the meetings.

Jerry reported that as time went on he felt more and more angry, but he could not figure out why. Joe had not done anything, said anything, or sent any negative notes to Jerry. The first verbal hint that something was wrong took place when Joe cornered Jerry in a hallway and made an accusation that Jerry was avoiding him. Jerry commented later that he really did not know how to react. He simply told Joe that that was not the case. Joe left Jerry in the hallway but remarked harshly as he walked away, "You better not be avoiding me."

Several people in an adjacent room heard the confrontation and later remarked to Jerry that a new part of Joe's personality was emerging. However, it was simply the stress that occurs when restructuring takes place. This too will pass, they said. They then advised Jerry not to worry about it. (This is an example of the denial that often takes place when something very wrong is happening within a department, or the entire organization for that matter.)

Jerry did his best not to avoid the new boss. In fact, Jerry began reporting some production problems that were starting to arise. Jerry did it without accusing anyone but by simply defining the actual problem. Joe would not respond but simply squinted his eyes at Jerry. Jerry began to feel he should not tell him about the problems.

Two weeks went by before Joe called Jerry into his office. He wanted to know why Jerry had not been reporting the production problems that were now in a definite growth pattern. The tone of voice was threatening and confusing to Jerry. He did not know how to answer because he did not want to tell Joe that his demeanor had sent the nonverbal message of, "You had better not tell me about those problems."

Jerry simply commented after a moment of silence, "Things have been super busy," while Joe gave him the eye-squinting routine.

Joe then ordered Jerry to report the problems or there would be consequences.

Two days later, Jerry went in to see Joe about a problem. This time, there was a new direction to the response. Joe asked, "If you know about these problems, why aren't you working to avoid them?" This was not Jerry's job. He was not a direct supervisor in the production department. He was experiencing a *Catch 22* from every direction.

Jerry's anger was increasing as time went on, and he wanted to avoid the VP at all possible costs. A few days later, Joe met Jerry in the hallway, and Joe was nice to him. He patted Jerry on the back and told him that he was great to work with. Jerry fell for the routine and reported a new problem two days later thinking that everything was okay. Instead, the VP screamed at Jerry and told Jerry that he was being watched.

Jerry requested a meeting with the president, which ended in total bewilderment. Jerry later indicated that he felt like a fool, a complete idiot, and unable to do an adequate job. He said that he had no self-esteem left. Worse yet, Jerry had gone to see the Employee Assistance Program (EAP) counselor, and he was simply told, "Buck up, it's simply job stress with the changes in the new management structure." (Even the EAP counselors can voice the same type of denial because of a lack of knowledge of this destructive technique.)

The newly overt, negative forces at work continued, and Jerry eventually had a nervous breakdown. No one understood what had happened! Jerry was a victim of a

> Dragon boss. He knew something was wrong but was never able to really define the problem. Now, he thought it was his own fault. This is exactly what the Dragon wanted him to think.

Jerry's story is not that unusual. He was totally confused and felt that something like this could not be happening. He was vulnerable, angry, and concerned about his career. If you are feeling this way, or you know someone who is in such a situation, it is time to get a clear picture of how these abusive bosses operate. It goes far beyond the classic bully routine.

How Dragons Abuse and Victimize

In order to become a human doormat, one must first lie down. Victims do not lie down easily and volunteer to be victimized. Therefore, human predators, from con artists and pedophiles to tyrants, disarm and groom their victims, gain their confidence, and then slowly take control of their lives.

During the Holocaust, for example, victims and bystanders were groomed by propaganda, information control, and persecution to surrender their freedom and their personal power to resist the unthinkable atrocities that were "secret" at the time. As every Dragon knows, terrified victims typically offer little resistance to the abuse of power. Even the pedophile grooms little victims with lollipop lures and deceptive kindness before innocent trust results in physical control and naivete turns to terror.

1. Grooming

At the first stages of grooming, most victims are vaguely aware of feeling angry (nature's automatic warning of impending danger), but any protests are typically silenced by denial. Being exposed to conflicting experiences, words, and grandiose promises usually confuses potential victims. A trusting or dependent relationship develops where the victim is trained to accept mild abuse without overt anger. The victim tries to stay on the predator's good side, keep the predator as a friend, and gain some sort of personal reward as well. The predator, on the other hand, offers false friendship, power, or material rewards as bait to lure the victim to proceed willingly to the second stage. The second stage is where a sorting-out process begins with reveled secrets and resulting pressures on the victim to remain silent.

The grooming stage has two objectives for Dragons:

- The Dragon is looking for individuals who will support dishonesty and/or the Dragon's inability to lead. If the person will not do so, it is an automatic setup for eventual dismissal.
- The Dragon has a need to destroy (not simply terminate) an individual who has a greater knowledge of the organization and is perceived by the Dragon as a threat, such as in Jerry's case previously mentioned.

This sets the stage for the setup!

2. The Setup

The abuser often exposes the "groomed target" to an immoral, illegal, life-threatening, or unethical secret, then informally tests the victim for loyalty. Using the victim's naivete, the abuser pressures the target into unwritten and unspoken ("don't blow-the-whistle") promises in exchange for personal gain. For "looking the other way," supporting the abuser, or being loyal to the "cause," the victim may be given reassuring words, protection, sex, friendship, or enticing promises of future rewards. Unfortunately, the fine print in their unwritten contract calls for surrendering freedom to the insatiable power needs of the Dragon.

Once a victim keeps the dark secret (to continue receiving rewards or to avoid punishment), the victim becomes the Dragon's pawn and must remain silent. Victims who support the cause must continue to do whatever the predator demands, including accepting abuse without complaint. If the victims fail their tests or break their silence, then attack, retaliation, and retribution are inevitable.

Potential victims who are emotionally healthy can count on their mixed feelings of confusion and anger to warn them that they are in danger. Dragons, however, counter such natural feelings with increased pressures that may range from the "offer-you-can't-resist" to violence. As they move their victims into their range of control where fear begins to surface, the abusers either force their victims into complete compliance or simply designate them as Dragon food. "Dragon food" is the victim who the Dragon sees as a threat and cannot or will not be brought into the Dragon's circle of Doorkeepers. People who are designated as Dragon food are used, abused, and eventually discarded.

3. The Hook

Most slaves, having no liberty, feel terror more intensely than anger. In this same way, victims seldom feel anger after they have been groomed. As abuse escalates and freedom is curtailed, victims feel confused, threatened, and terrorized. Confusion – generated by simultaneous but opposing feelings and thoughts – clouds decision-making ability and lessens the chances of escaping from the abuse.

Victims become obsessed with surviving emotionally as well as physically. Some lose their sense of self-determination and simply stop thinking. They may accept their abusers as a special sort of deity and follow along like cult members. Those who are able to cut through their confusion often find that their lives have been altered significantly. In the third stage of victimization, the Dragon hooks victims by pressuring them into participating in their nefarious activities, thus assuring their victims' cooperation.

Some people are not willing to participate in the Dragon's devious schemes. These people must be dealt with differently. For those victims who are a threat to the boss because of their work quality, knowledge, positive relationships, and unwillingness to participate in dishonesty, the hook stage is designed to destroy all will to fight back and recover. Thus, Lord Acton's dictum holds true, "*Power corrupts. Absolute power corrupts absolutely.*"

The generic-style bully is no stranger to the business world. Bullies are especially attracted to management or power positions. In the business and political worlds, some executives are tempted to cross the line from demanding results to occasionally abusing their power. However, we are not dealing with generic bullies; we are dealing with Dragons.

Dragons are those abusers who display narcissistic tendencies and have a grandiose sense of self-importance and entitlement. They bask in power and enjoy subjugating others to their control through manipulation, intimidation, and threats. To ensure dominance, they demand extraordinary personal sacrifices from employees. In addition to verbal abuse, they subject targeted employees to workplace isolation, personal humiliation, and economic stress. All of these manipulations are part of the boss's unwritten, "fine-print" conditions for continued employment, or *perceived* continued employment on the part of the victim who is targeted for constructive dismissal and does not yet know it. In general, the higher up the power ladder the executive is, the more abusive practices are tolerated and the less the behavior is questioned.

But why does workplace abuse seem so crazy, so confusing to the victim? Similar to other types of abuse, it is a secret! Grooming is done so skillfully that most victims do not realize what has occurred. They disregard any anger warnings as inappropriate and any of their suspicions as misinterpretations of the boss's motives. Although a few may sense at some level that something is wrong, most people simply want to believe that the boss is credible, honorable, and has their best interests at heart.

> George provided a typical example of denial in this type of situation. He felt that the bosses wanted to get rid of him, but he continually denied this by saying to himself, "Why would they want to get rid of me when they sent me to New York to correct the loss of customers?" Actually, the assignment in New York was a ploy

> to get George out of the way for a period of time, and they hoped that he would fail with the assignment.
>
> George did not realize that his success in regaining the customers was a new level of threat to his Dragon boss, who wanted to get rid of George so that other dishonest activities within the company would remain undetected. George was then subjected to a long-term, destructive mystification process designed to create failure and a reason for dismissal – if he didn't simply resign because of the overt campaign of stress placed upon him.

Employees are gradually groomed to tiptoe around the abuser's office where there is yelling, tears, or questionable activity occurring. By the time the second stage of victimization is complete, they deny that they have been abused, have heard tales of harassment, or that they witnessed questionable practices within the workplace. They learn that in this setting the term "business ethics" is an oxymoron and that anyone who brings a problem to the boss *is the problem.* They fear that unless they remain silent, public humiliation followed by termination is inevitable, no matter what it takes to accomplish the deed.

Ironically, outward appearances reflect the opposite of reality. Victims appear to be bringing disfavor (and, of course, humiliation and termination) upon themselves, while the boss appears to be legitimately strong and in control, simply doing an unpleasant job that has to be done. This is part of the mystification process.

There are major differences between Dragons and productive managers. There are also major differences between the management styles of healthy organizations and the abusive styles that support a Dragon in the workplace. Using intimidation, secrecy, and denial, Dragons deliberately mystify the workplace. Newly hired abusers have been known to declare artificial emergencies and create chaos merely to gain and maintain control of their victims.

Any boss or any employee can lose control in an angry moment. That seems to be one of our human frailties. But Dragon behavior is not the same as inadvertent harshness. It is not the same as conflict, disagreement, and the arbitration processes occurring in most healthy organizations. Abuse in the hands of a Dragon is a destructive pattern of predictable behaviors that exist solely to feed the insatiable personal hunger of one individual. Driven by their own immense emotional needs to a preoccupation with power and control, Dragons are elusive predators who stalk their victims secretly. Often, the very organizations that unwittingly support a Dragon's existence end up being victimized as well. The boss is without conscience and when trapped will attack, without mercy, anyone or anything that gets in the way.

Productive managers attack problems. Dragons attack people. The central theme of workplace abuse, although never admitted, is the subjugation of people to satisfy the selfish wants and needs of the Dragon, whether or not it is in the best interests of the organization. When the predator is feeding from within, organizational goals get lost. Needs of customers, clients, students, stockholders, employees, and voters – the very purpose of the organization's existence – disappear as the employee (the victim) struggles to survive each day.

As for the workers, it is not until they begin to sense danger and notice that they have been hooked into a dysfunctional system of secrecy, cover up, and blame that they reach out for support. Often, support is unproductive simply because many professionals do not yet recognize "Dragon tracks," or abusers' signature patterns and techniques. Such abuse continues to be confused with *job stress* and is accepted as simply part of the job. Insightful victims who successfully cut through workplace mystification must then make major career decisions and changes or remain as pawns for the Dragon.

Dragon tactics and strategies are denied, sometimes vigorously. The following example is about a person who tried to report a strategy that she overheard while at her desk near the office door of her boss. She did not know at the time that this person was a Dragon.

> Diane was an executive secretary to an assistant vice president (and Dragon) for a company that paid bonuses to management based on cost reports. This arrangement created destructive, interdepartmental competition rather than a positive, collaborative working climate. One afternoon, she was shocked to overhear her boss hatch a scheme with a middle-management-level supervisor to eliminate Tom, a department manager.
>
> Diane was confused and bewildered by what she had heard because she knew Tom to be honest, kind, and hardworking. He was the type of person who got along well with everyone, and he was about to qualify for a substantial bonus based on his successful cost/revenue ratio for his department. (Tom's success and working relationship with customers and staff was a threat to the AVP.)
>
> "The real problem," said the AVP, "is that Tom doesn't compete with other departments. He's too nice. He's a threat [to us]. This is what I want you to do." The AVP went on to give instructions that were classic Dragon ploys. (See Steps II and IV.)
>
> According to Diane's notes, the list of dirty deeds went something like this:

Dragon Deeds

- Set him up by asking "Why did you . . . ?"
- Demand the opposite of whatever he is doing to make him feel like a fool.

- Cut him out of the information loop but do not let him know about it.
- Make sure he misses meetings; take his name off the list and blame Diane.
- Put on the pressure but cut his budget.
- Make him fail. Show him who the boss is around here.
- Load his file with reprimands but do not mention them to him.

The list went on and on. Realizing that her boss was a Dragon, she decided to report the incident to the Vice President. He responded, "Jack (the AVP) would never do anything like that. You must be mistaken." So much for trying to help the corporation!

Still reeling after her rebuff from the VP, she shared her entire, amazing story with her business administration class at a nearby university. The professor then stated before the entire class, "No one who has reached such a powerful position in management would do anything like that!" The power and status of the Dragon mystified even her professor. The professor concluded, "No manager in his position would be so callous! You must not have all the facts straight."

Not having been believed twice by respectable authority figures, she questioned her own observations. Without support, she kept quiet. She remained loyal until, under extreme pressures at work, she too felt victimized and depleted by her boss's excessive demands.

Diane resigned, citing "job stress" as her reason, and then entered therapy for depression. In therapy, she learned about abuse, dealt with her feelings, and put her career back together. Later, she changed universities and completed a graduate degree in business administration.

> Diane had seen through the mystification, but no one believed her.

Meanwhile, the AVP went on to target many people throughout the next few years, and no one understood what was happening. He was praised for his take-charge leadership, but he drove many good employees and customers away. Finally, decaying from within, the company failed.

If this individual, closed-office strategy for destruction and constructive dismissal shocks you, be aware that it happens more often than people want to admit. In fact, these methods are even discussed within group instruction and seminars. Some Dragon managers feel that unless you are firing people, you are not doing your job. Seminars are held on how to do it!

> A middle manager, Jennifer, was under a great deal of stress because she had not been firing people in her department. She repeatedly explained that her staff was doing an excellent job and that morale was high. She pointed out that the value of the work staff went far beyond the payroll costs and that, therefore, the staff was an important asset to the company. She noted that there was not a single person within the staff that should be fired.
>
> A few weeks later, the middle managers were sent to a seminar held by the company on how to fire a person you do not like but cannot simply dismiss because of positive customer relations or many other reasons. It was an eight-hour session on how to start nitpicking on normal, everyday errors with the goal of increasing stress for the targeted employee. The stress in turn will create other errors, mistakes, misjudgments, and destroy the person's self-confidence and will to fight back. Thus, a new level of poor performance can be used for dismissal, and it appears as though it is the employee's

own fault. These were the specific words used in this company seminar!

This is a story that some people simply refuse to believe. Such seminars are held regularly by organizations that are under the control of Dragons. Many times, the process is shrouded with such interesting words as "teamwork" and "site-based decision making," which create the allusion that the seminar is for a different objective. However, words that give away the real objective include: "If you are unwilling to embrace the new management's systems, you will have to get off the bus," and "If you cannot change, you better start looking for a new job right now." Sometimes the words are said with such sweetness that people actually think that the bosses are teasing to inject humor in the seminar. Such humor must be laid to rest!

Are You Feeling Job Stress or Victimization?

It is important to recognize the differences between normal job stress and the extreme stress generated by abuse in the workplace. Not only is the latter very uncomfortable, but it can be destructive to your physical health and your psychological well-being. Victimization has no place in a healthy environment. No one should be forced to tolerate abuse in order to earn a living.

Only dysfunctional organizations support Dragons in the workplace. Healthy organizations, which offer no haven for Dragons, rid themselves of power-drunk abusers when they spot Dragon tracks and expose abusive manipulations. The first task for employees and employers is to be alert. Learn what you need to know about how Dragons victimize and begin doing something to stop abuse. This requires documentation. Next, we will discuss how to get started.

Summary

- Dragon bosses select people for destruction because of high-quality work and organizational knowledge. These employees are threatening to the boss but cannot simply be fired.
- Classic victimization is done in three stages: Grooming, the Setup, and the Hook.
- Victims are groomed, silenced, and hooked.
- The workplace is not immune to abuse and victimization.
- Abuse of power creates victims.
- Dragons need victims in order to feed an insatiable appetite for power.
- Everyone surrounding Dragons eventually becomes victimized, including the organization that supports them.
- Victims operate under extreme stress, fear, shame, and confusion.
- Workplace Dragons create chaos in an atmosphere of hate and greed to promote destructive competition while they assume total power and control.
- Dragons operate in a mystified atmosphere of secrecy, denial, and silence.
- Dragons cannot survive in a healthy workplace environment.
- Healthy employees cannot survive with Dragons.
- Dragons are extremely resistant to change.
- Be aware of your own vulnerability to mystification by:
    - a. recognizing and honoring your insights
    - b. cutting through your own denial
    - c. looking for objective evidence to support or refute your suspicion that a Dragon might be lurking in your workplace
    - d. remember to document in detail (See Chapter 2.)

Questions for Reflection

After reviewing workplace experiences in this chapter, discuss the following questions:

1. How do these stories compare with your experiences?
2. Does the information in the stories remind you of anyone else you know?
3. How can naivete and denial play a part in keeping victims of workplace abuse trapped within a dysfunctional organization?
4. What are some of the choices that victims have, and what are some of the possible consequences that might follow from those decisions?

Chapter 2

What You Need to Know to Get Started

You now have an idea of some of the abusive tactics used in the workplace, but in order to survive and grow, you will have to do something about the problem. To start with, ***document everything***!

After proofreading our manuscript, Frank commented, "I wish that I had known this when I was forced out of my job twelve years ago! Now I can pick out the Dragon tracks, but at that time, I didn't see any options. Furthermore, I never documented anything. All I have is a file folder of miscellaneous memos. Why didn't you write this book years ago when I needed it? I would never have put myself through that torture! No wonder the company went out of business. The picture is so clear now! I guess that's called being too smart, too late, isn't it?"

We want you to be smart now, not when it is too late to do you any good. So, do not wait until you finish this book. Start documenting everything now, and this is how to do it: keep a Dragon diary (DD). Forget about your computer for this job, it simply will not do. We want this record to be handwritten, noted according to the time of incidents, and supported with your own personal file that is stored at home, not in your workplace.

Set your DD in a dated format, one or more pages per day as needed. Use a spiral or hard-bound notebook, not a loose-leaf one. The reason for this is that once confronted, your Dragon may make accusations that you inserted new pages in order to falsify records in some manner. Keep your basic records in dark, indelible ink but have colored pens available for adding comments, questions, or insights as you go.

Although your diary is sure to vary according to your particular situation, using the following general format is a good way to get started. There is always an urge to procrastinate, especially when you do not know exactly what to write and when the words you need to use are often psychologically painful to acknowledge.

1. Use the first page or so for history. Describe your work situation, as well as what has happened to cause you concern regarding your career.
2. Be sure to keep unbiased notes by recording positive, negative, and neutral events as they happen. Document them as follows:
    - Incident
    - What happened? (Be as objective as you can.)
    - When and where? (Date, time of day, and location)
    - Who was there? (Name participants, witnesses, and bystanders.)
    - Written documents (or relevant filed data that supports this incident)
    - Why? (Include your best guess, hypothesis, comments, your reasoning, and thoughts about the incident.)
3. As you read through this book and acquire more insight into what may be happening within your workplace, you will want to add personal comments on feelings, thoughts, or conclusions to your diary, sometimes in retrospect. Leave space between incidents and in the margins of each page for notes. Choose pens of varying colors for your comments or "asides" and be sure to date your additions accordingly. For example, after reading through the chapters in Step III, you might use a red pen to represent your emotional state at a time when you felt angry but later realized that you were really quite frightened. After reading Step IV, thinking rationally about past emotional incidents, and making your future plans, you might return to your DD and add more recent comments in green ink to represent your calm, rational reassessment of the previous events.

Keeping a record of the abusive events can be extremely painful. Lisa, an administrative assistant in

> Illinois, reported that her boss had approached her for sexual favors. She refused, and of course, he told her that if she told anyone about it, she would not be believed. After all, he had thirty years with the organization. Lisa indicated that for a while nothing extreme happened except for his negative body language. About three months later, the boss began to make life difficult with a wide variety of nit-picking, which increased in frequency over time. She decided to keep a dairy of the events that took place. However, after two months, it became so painful to write that she simply gave up on her documentation.
>
> Lisa thought the only thing to do was to request a transfer. It took about three months, but she was finally granted her request. On her last day with the abusive Dragon, he called her in and told her, "You're leaving now, but our paths will cross again." Three months later, her Dragon was reassigned to her new division, and he became her boss again.

We cannot emphasize enough the importance of documentation, no matter how painful the process may be. Ultimately, it would have been invaluable for Lisa, especially with her boss's transfer to her new division. In one case, documentation paid off for a woman who had been subjected to a substantial amount of abuse. She took the documentation to Human Resources, and the abuser was dismissed. Fortunately, this company did not have an inner circle of Dragons controlling every part of the organization.

As you read Step II on how to identify and unmask the Dragon, we hope that you will find the information enlightening. With new insights about workplace abuse, you can move along the precarious path between paranoia and persecution to a safe place where you can confidently say, "My boss is or is not a dragon, and this is what I can do about it!"

Step II

Unmask the Dragon

Dragons operate in secret. Smooth and manipulative, they are often masked by the public perception of respectability. They seldom disclose their predatory ways in the presence of more powerful people. Part of the victims' confusion lies in sorting out just who is the Dragon and which employees are Doorkeepers protecting the Dragon's interests and actual identity.

Step II shows how to identify Dragons in your workplace by their "six signature patterns of behavior." Furthermore, we list and demonstrate some of the most common diabolical games that Dragons and their supporters enjoy playing at the expense of their victims and the organization.

As you become familiar with the power plays in your work setting, you will not only be able to spot the Dragon, but you will learn how to track and anticipate the next attack. Armed with such knowledge, it is possible to avoid the dirty tricks and fight the intimidation. You may even learn to enjoy the challenge of tracking a Dragon as you weigh your options and plan your future.

Chapter 3
Dragon Tracking

How to Identify a Dragon Boss

It may appear as though Dragon bosses have trained for their abusive techniques. They have become experts in the exploitative use of power, control, and intimidation. Although the backgrounds and the specific settings in which they operate include the home, the streets, the gang, the political arena, and the workplace, abusers have many commonalties.

They have a love-hate relationship with terror. They harbor deep-seated fears of their own but admire abusive tactics used to intimidate, overpower, and terrorize those under their domination. They often give lip service to the concepts of dignity and respect. However, they react to dignity as if it were a character flaw and consider gaining respect as their license to terrorize. Being excellent manipulators, they typically mouth the correct words at the correct time, but their true identity lies not in what they say but in what they do.

Just as we can identify the species of an animal that has raided a campsite by its footprints, droppings, odors, and characteristic patterns of destruction, one can identify a Dragon by its tracks. We can identify the presence of a workplace Dragon by the "six signature patterns" that spell out its name:

D for Deception

R for Relationships

A for Assessment

G for Grooming

O for Ostracizing

N for Numbing

These abusers are psychologically needy individuals. They have personality characteristics that require rather intensive attention to their own insecurities through the use of power and control tactics. They exhibit many of the following characteristics.
Dragons typically:

- have experienced exposure to a pathological abuse/victim relationship early in life
- do not trust others
- are confused by sincerity or emotions
- are constantly manipulating
- secretly feel that others control their destiny
- have poor self-esteem but hide it even from themselves
- believe people are friends only as long as they stay and tolerate abuse without question
- secretly fear abandonment
- believe they must be in control to be safe
- see respect as that which follows punishment
- feel sexy and in control after defeating someone
- have a rigid and polarized outlook on life
- can compartmentalize their lives
- are resistant to change
- have a secret life that allows special privileges and harbor grandiose delusions either secretly or openly
- are hyper-vigilant and defensive about their personal lives; refuse to look at self

Signature Pattern No. 1: Deception

Dragons are masters at lying and thrive on chaos. Throwing people off balance gives them a decided advantage. If the organization is not already in crisis, they will create one. In any panic situation, new leadership is unquestioned. Even grossly abusive behavior is tolerated as a necessary evil under the misguided notion that this too will pass. No matter what move the Dragon makes, any negative result can be attributed to someone else. Deception is easily accomplished by a fake emergency that features rapid changes and frenzied innovations. Unwarranted changes for the sake of chaos are one of the costly aspects of a Dragon's prowling in any organization.

Organizations often employ these manipulators because of the number of innovations found in their resume. Although a resume might look great, half-truths and misinformation often hide the facts regarding the person's negative impact on the former company. As masterful manipulators, Dragons are charismatic and grooming typically begins with the interview committee being the first victims. It is a rare search group that thinks to check with not just the most recent employer but two or more previous employers regarding the value of those innovations or their effects upon the organization after the candidate has departed.

> One such Dragon, Andy, left a trail of innovative management systems. He went from one organization to another and was welcomed for his record of having instituted rapid changes. Had interviewers recognized a signature pattern, they could have checked his background and noted that with each move his innovations had nothing to do with company, customer, or client needs. Such information is hard to gather, however, because those left in the wake of destructive changes are either still mystified, in denial, or embarrassed by having been taken in. Even former supervisors who are well aware of the Dragon's destructive impact may provide credible recommendations simply to hasten that person's departure.
>
> Andy typically moved into an organization at a senior-management level and instantly created a whirlwind of activity. Committees, seminars, training sessions, and new work schedules were implemented. Confusion ensued after management gave lip service to changes that they really did not support, much to the

delight of the Dragon. At each career move, chaos was established, throwing the staffs off balance and leaving Andy in charge with total power. What the Board of Directors did not notice, however, were the fingers he pointed at his new victims for undermining his innovations. Andy typically gathered great recommendations and moved on to more powerful positions, all the while leaving a wake of chaos behind as he departed.

Sometimes, these manipulators initiate sweeping changes and are confronted with questions regarding how changes impact clients, customers, or employees. One standard dodge is, "It is irrelevant to ask questions or to look at where we have been. Our goal is to move forward rapidly without wasting time." Typically, Dragons downsize (which is perceived as a brilliant cost reduction), cut the research budget, and discredit research results by saying, "You can prove anything with statistics." Ironically, the Dragon uses statistics for the downsizing with the secret agenda of creating chaos.

Besides dodging relevant questions, these bosses use propaganda and misinformation to their advantage. They feel no pangs of conscience as they stretch the truth, withhold vital information, obstruct justice, or simply deliver bold-faced lies. They have been known to initiate false charges and investigations about a victim's character just to discredit that person. The charges and the investigations are always listed in the victim's file but never the follow-up information that notes that the charges were unfounded or that investigations supported the defendant's innocence. Other Dragons simply insert undocumented suspicions in their unsuspecting victims' files. When and if any victims ask to see their personnel files, a typical distraction maneuver is performed giving the Dragon time to change or cover up the deceit.

Manipulative bosses have been known to reveal gossip about the organization or targeted employees while extracting loyalty promises from the listener by saying, "This is just between us, and if you ever tell anyone that I told you, I will say that you lied." (See Game No. 2, Chapter 4.)

Dragons are so comfortable in stretching the truth that they often delude themselves and appear to believe that their lies are actually true. Their charismatic qualities often make it incredibly difficult not to believe the assertions. The bigger the lie, the more it is accepted by the victims, stockholders, clients, customers, and often the general public. Two examples of how some Dragon managers have set people up for dismissal is through the expense accounts. In one case, a Dragon told his assistant to include various items in the assistant's expense account, which he would later pay back to the Dragon after being reimbursed. The assistant, wrongly thinking he should do what the boss wanted, went ahead with the request. Later when auditors examined the victim's expense account requests, he was fired for his dishonesty. The Dragon looked good because he had pointed out the dishonest event.

In the other case, a Dragon manager had made the same type of request to a staff member. The staff member refused, and because she had not gone along with the dishonest venture, she was then singled out for constructive dismissal. The Dragon used strategic techniques to make it appear that the termination was her fault.

Occasionally, Dragons become entrapped by their own lies. When truth begins to unravel their deceptive practices, they put on quite a show. Like ensnared alligators, they twist, turn, and roll in all directions to escape taking responsibility for their deception. When cornered, they can become quite vicious. Their classic defense is always an unbridled attack. Anyone or any organization that openly pursues a Dragon is considered fair game for them and their Doorkeepers. Regardless of the consequences to themselves, the organization, or its goals and reputation, a true Dragon persists as though it were a life-and-death struggle. Unfortunately, in some rare cases, such aggression can lead to injury and even death. The most common outcome, however, is that the Dragons win the struggle, advance in their careers, and move on to prey upon another organization ready and willing to be groomed and mystified.

Victims, as well as Doorkeepers, may find themselves deeply involved in legal or personal problems and on a roller coaster of emotions that often calls for therapy. They are also forced to consider unplanned career changes. Those people who are knowledgeable about tracking Dragons rarely succumb to the emotional ride. They can simply prepare themselves for the expected attacks (See Steps III and IV). Then they are ready to stand aside while the truth about the deception becomes the Dragon's own trap.

Signature Pattern No. 2: Relationships

Dragons approach relationships with employees in much the same fashion as a predator toward prey. They use people and feel lost without victims. They deliberately create an environment conducive to symbiotic abuse/victim relationships where they can build their power base and feed their desire for control.

When tracking a lion, one looks for its den and the remains of its prey. When tracking a Dragon in the workplace, one should look for the Doorkeepers who create a safe den for a powerful Dragon and then search for the victims who remain. But let us clarify this just a bit; what you think you see is not always what is true. Let's look first at the victims and how they play out their roles in protecting the dysfunctional workplace.

These predators cannot survive long without victims to support their appetites for power and control. These victims, we will call them Doormats for the time being, come in two varieties, the true victims and the false ones. Dragons do not care on which variety they trample.

True Doormats are people who trust unconditionally. They are sincere workers who have always conducted their business practices ethically. Accustomed to accepting authority, truthful, and non-rebellious, they are easily intimidated and silenced. They are only concerned about keeping their jobs. Some true Doormats may come from abusive backgrounds where they learned to take orders and disparaging comments without flinching. They believe that their jobs are on the line unless they are willing to accept abuse while remaining respectful, reliable, and in awe of their boss's power. Easily bullied, these people enter the workplace as prime targets for any Dragon's power. Unfortunately, they are no match for such predators. Doormats stay on the job until drained of all their emotional energy and resources.

Then there are the false Doormats. They may be naive but seldom are they sincere. They are often Dragons-in-waiting. These opportunists may be perceived as victims, but they are secretly interning under the Dragon, anticipating the chance to outdo the boss and take over. They are willingly groomed and hooked into Dragon/Doormat relationships by their own greed and lust for power.

The boldest of the false Doormat group may actually out manipulate their bosses. They eagerly agree to become victims as well as supporters, as long as they are free to abuse others and profit from the boss's secret activities. Since they are less like a Doormat than they are like a henchman or bodyguard, we call these hybrid Doormats the Doorkeepers. They typically front for the true Dragon, who often keeps a low profile. Stockholders and the outside world may even see the boss as kindly, generous, thoughtful, and incapable of such abuses and manipulations.

In the end, however, most Doorkeepers suffer the same fate as true Doormats. They are exploited and have their careers ruined in service to the Dragon. Many are scapegoats for the boss's activities, and if the situation is serious enough, some are even arrested. Some go into therapy, and a few actually take their lives rather than face the consequences of their naivete. Almost always, they damage their own reputations and lives and have a hard time climbing back to where they once were.

Doorkeepers usually stay with the firm until the Dragon is exposed or leaves. Then they desperately try to cover their tracks. Used, abused, and then abandoned by their bosses, Doorkeepers typically search frantically for another Dragon to serve. Rarely do they move into the boss's empty office unless the organization is still in denial.

Signature Pattern No. 3: Assessment

Dragons do not choose Doorkeepers or victims at random; they select them. If a Dragon manager believes that an individual has a higher intelligence or a greater knowledge about the organization and its clients or customers, that person is immediately selected for victimization. On the other hand, if the Dragon feels as though a person would be a Doorkeeper, that person is tested through an informal, situational assessment typically executed with such care that the individual rarely recognizes what has taken place. You may have unknowingly witnessed such an event if there is a Dragon in your workplace. Those who pass the test are selected for grooming as Doorkeepers, while those who fail are slated to become Doormats, victims to be devoured as needed to keep the system going.

The Test:

This four-part test determines whether or not the unsuspecting candidate for grooming is willing to:

1. Go along with being placed in a vulnerable position
2. Engage in or witness some sort of deviant behavior
3. Keep silent about the Dragon's manipulations
4. Protect the Dragon and the established system of power plays

Scoring Key:
There are 25 points for each section. A perfect score is 100%.

- 100% You passed.
You will be groomed as a Doorkeeper and be promised unlimited power to control and abuse others as long as you protect the Dragon. A perfect score entitles you to become an insider. Perks and protection, as well as punishments, are part of the contract and will surely be awarded according to the Dragon's whims.

- 75% You passed.
You are a candidate for advancement to Doorkeeper. You will be "watched" carefully as a Doorkeeper-in-waiting. You will most certainly be abused in the process, but you will be supported by the Dragon and given privileges as long as you do as you are told and keep quiet.

- 50% You failed in the Dragon's eyes.
This means that you are on the waiting list to be set up, abused, and manipulated. As a regular victim, you will be devoured only when you are no longer of use to the boss or when you break your silence about the secret activities.

- 25% You failed.
You are to be a candidate for Dragon food. Most likely, you will be portrayed as a slow banquet for all to nibble on, especially if your credentials are impeccable and your early departure would cast suspicion on the Dragon.

- 0% You failed.
Failing the test results in being designated by the Dragon as either "fast food," where you lose your job immediately, or as a banquet to be abused by the system and then tossed out at a later date. If you don't resign on your own, you will be pressured until you do.

The following classic examples illustrate how the administration of the test can involve a variety of situations and locations.

As a new faculty member, Juan was subjected to an encounter with prostitutes during an out-of-state professional meeting with senior members. He silently withdrew and surrounded himself with professional colleagues as protection. Being untenured and vulnerable, he failed parts 1 and 2 of the test by refusing to participate in or witness the behavior but passed parts 3 and 4 by keeping silent and protecting the Dragon and the system with his silence. He earned 50 points out of 100.

With a score of 50 percent, Juan was unknowingly slated for grooming as a true Doormat. As long as the system remained dysfunctional, he had little hope of advancement. In order to keep his job he would need to:

- "Agree" to be abused verbally
- Keep silent and protect the Dragon's secrets

If and when Juan decided to protest against the Dragon's abuses of himself or others, he would be moved as a victim directly into the Dragon food category and strategically destroyed by the Doorkeepers under the protection of the Dragon and others in the system.

Charnel was declared the designated driver by a group of managers who let their hair down one night. She was subjected to obscene language and backbiting, with the managers sharing personal information about others in the company. She would not join in the character assassinations or the partying. She refused to attend other out-of-town meetings with the group and was clear in stating her displeasure with their behavior.

When given orders to abuse others under her managerial control, she dragged her feet. The Dragon went to the district manager with tales that Charnel could not be trusted because she questioned forthcoming policy changes. The Dragon said that she might not be a *cooperative team member* for the company.

With a Score of "0," Charnel was to become Dragon food because she:

- Would not go along with unethical behavior and partying.
- Refused to witness this type of behavior.
- Did not keep quiet about the matter.
- Would not protect a perverse system.

Her credentials were excellent and the company needed her expertise. Therefore, the process of removing Charnel from the company would take some time. She had to be removed, however, because she was clearly a threat to the Dragon. Charnel was harassed until she resigned. She sued for sexual harassment but lost her claim because she had no documentation to prove that she had filed a formal complaint with the company. The court stated that she had not given the company adequate opportunity to rectify the problem before she resigned.

As you can see from these examples, passing three or four requirements on the test gives the candidate access to power and control as a future Doorkeeper, a Dragon-in-training. Doorkeepers admire Dragons and attempt to protect and promote the exploitative climate created by them. Ethical, responsible, morally principled employees almost invariably earn less than 50 percent and are slated for Dragon food.

This sort of informal testing goes on in some very powerful companies. This is especially the case when there has been no sensitivity training, and the management is supportive of a competitive atmosphere between and among departments and staff members. If

Dragons have taken over the management systems of an organization, the testing of new staff members can be extreme and sometimes very vicious. It is no longer a question of how threatening a highly successful staff member might be but rather how the power-driven culture can continue to be expanded. Potential threats to the power culture are often weeded out during the initial interview process. Subsequently, new staff members who have already passed the Dragon's interview techniques are exposed to gross intimidation literally on the first day of the new job.

Signature Pattern No. 4: Grooming

Just as a fire cannot exist without oxygen, this abuse cannot exist if it is suffocated. Recognized and confronted correctly, the fiery breath of one lone Dragon in a healthy organization would be quickly extinguished. So, the first step an alert Dragon takes when attaining power is cutting the odds of being extinguished by *creating a support group of Doorkeepers* to keep the Doormats and others in line.

Grooming in the workplace is a continuous three-stage process of recruiting Doorkeepers and Doormats, as well as setting people up for immediate victim status. All abusers know what grooming is, from the Dragon who entices with promises of promotion to the domestic abuser who utters kind words of apology with gifts and promises to stop the hitting. The pattern is the same!

Workplace grooming involves hints of unlimited success, social contacts, gaining access to private inside information that will assure advancements, fabulous expense accounts, perks, fantastic salaries, bonuses, and the like. But in order to remain on the good side of the boss, one must put up with "just a little abuse." The trade off seems to be an obvious choice to the victim. The lures appear so enticing that anyone would willingly take a little abuse in the exchange. In this case, the purpose of the abuse is to send the message that the Dragon always has the power, and in a strange way, the Dragon is demonstrating a lack of full trust in the new Doorkeeper.

By the time the recruit has become entranced with the lures and comfortable with the abuse, that person is set up with an exciting confidence involving something that may be illegal, immoral, or unethical. To the natural risk taker - who has a taste for such larceny and subterfuge in the blood - the secret, deviant behavior, such as undercover deals or unearned power perks and privileges, is very appealing. These dealings are often done under an "it's good for the company" facade.

Once exposed to the information, the potential Doorkeepers/victims are involved in the Dragon's schemes. Having been intimidated by their previous exposure to abusive practices, they feel pressured to keep quiet. Whether they join in the questionable business activities or they remain silent and support it, they know that their careers are on the line.

If they succumb to temptation by joining in with the Dragons (keeping the big secret and doing as they are told), they are hooked. At this point, they are tested and delegated power, which is limited by the whims of the boss. They may or may not achieve their career goals, but by becoming part of the secret, they have surrendered their freedom. Once hooked, it is very difficult, if not impossible, to escape without being hurt in the process. Pressure, stress, intimidation, humiliation, and often terror are the rewards for remaining under the domination of a Dragon, which can happen in any field of work.

> Upon entering the hotel suite, Sandi, an intern psychologist, was shocked to see her abusive supervisor lying nude on the bed gesturing for Sandi to come join her. The intern quickly excused herself and left the convention with a polite explanation about a sudden emergency requiring her to return home immediately.
>
> Sandi recognized grooming when she experienced it. Her supervisor had come on to her inappropriately in a sexually explicit manner. Without uttering

a word, the supervisor let Sandi in on her secret, her sexual expectations, and had put the intern under her control. If Sandi kept the supervisor's confidence, she would probably be safe, and her internship would be secure, but she would probably never be considered for a full-time position. If she responded to the advance, she would be setting herself up for further sexual exploitation. She reviewed her options:

- If she reported her supervisor's sexual overtures to management, she thought no one would believe her. The supervisor, who enjoyed intimidating people, had all the power. There were no words spoken, so she could not quote the supervisor's exact words to anyone.
- If she resisted further invitations, she would be a candidate for emotional abuse.
- If she resigned, she would suffer economically.
- If she confronted the supervisor, the incident would surely be denied. And worse yet, she could be blamed for making the sexual advances to her supervisor!
- If she said nothing, the supervisor might misinterpret her silence as a victim's stance. Therefore, she could expect to be abused in other ways during her internship.

Sandi is not alone. She had been identified as a recruit for a Dragon who probably had a pattern of setting people up for the victim status. To Sandi, it seemed to be a lose-lose situation. She could either:

1. Comply with what the Dragon wanted, keep the job, and be exploited.
2. Reject the Dragon's wishes and be forced to leave or be abused.

Sandi realized how to handle the situation. She knew that she must pick her own time, make an appointment with her supervisor, and speak with her, making sure that the supervisor understood clearly that Sandi wanted to retain her internship but was unwilling to become involved in any sort of intimate relationship.

Sandi recognized a Dragon when she met one. She realized that she was being groomed and that she should expect to be attacked, threatened, and abused if she confronted the Dragon in the way one would normally confront any other supervisor. She also knew that these abusers existed in dysfunctional work settings. Sandi consulted with her university supervisor about her observations and conclusions and then transferred her internship to a healthy work setting.

Dragons typically groom Doorkeepers to become involved in symbiotic relationships, with the balance of power always in the Dragons' hands. Doorkeepers maintain their power only by accepting the abuse, but the key to the intimidating relationship is always a confidence, a secret that the victim silently agrees to guard.

When the secret involves sex and when one of the partners holds excessive power, it is considered abusive if that power is used to force the partner into compliance. When the powerful one is a Dragon and the partner a Doorkeeper, the balance of power can shift dramatically. Dragons offer power as their lure and Doorkeepers, opportunists that they are, eagerly look forward to being victims. By trading sex for power (and secret control over the Dragon), the victim appears to be helpless – simply pressured to comply with the demands. However, Doorkeepers usually have secret agendas of their own. They begin to groom their bosses in order to advance their own careers, to gather expensive gifts, to intimidate by threatening to expose the secret, or a number of other motives.

Unfortunately most Doorkeepers do not realize how deeply they are involved until they are hooked and victimized by their own compliant behavior. Although they know that their unwritten and typically unspoken contract for silence includes the risk of consequences, they believe that they have been granted unique privileges and can escape detection. Sadly, they typically suffer the same fate as true victims when the affair is over. When the abuser no longer has use for them, they are discarded. When they break the confidence, they are attacked without mercy. Dragons and their supporters may attempt to destroy their victims' careers, financial status, reputations, family harmony, emotional and physical well-being, personal safety, and often their actual freedom.

Signature Pattern No. 5: Ostracizing

Dragons are not necessarily crazy; they know exactly what they are doing and can be dangerous. They are experts at isolation and exclusion tactics. Ostracizing a victim is a pattern that can often be traced back to the abuser's earliest social relationships.

> Troy, a playground bully, typically greeted the other children with, "Hello Leo, hello Dennis, hello Marge, hello Shit." Taking their cue from the bully, the group excluded the victim, Shit, from their social gatherings.

Thus, the little bully began early in life to experience pleasure in emotionally dehumanizing young victims through isolation and exclusion tactics. At the work site, isolation is accomplished by ostracizing. Dragon Troy worked for a transport company and achieved management status relatively quickly in his career. He also knew when to use curse words as greetings and when to use a demeaning tone of voice that would cause other employees to pull away from the designated victim. Furthermore, when he called a meeting, he deliberately placed his victim in impossible situations by requesting information that the victim could not possibly know.

Troy would explain to the group that "so-and-so" was irresponsible and capable of causing severe embarrassment to the company. He would then place a formal reprimand in the victim's file.

If the victim summoned the courage to challenge Troy, the victim received, either publicly or privately, a loud and intimidating barrage of insults, such as "What the hell is wrong with you anyway? Are you crazy? Can you read, you #@&?" This counterattack would deplete the victim's self-confidence, forcing further social withdrawal and isolation.

There are several systems of ostracizing:

- Nguyen's first inkling of exclusion came when he found that his office had been moved during the weekend to a small closet-like space with no windows, next to the noisy elevator.
- Dana was moved to an outer office without walls completely exposed to hallway traffic.
- John was the subject of subtle name-calling after his office was moved.
- One victim, on the day he was leaving employment, was told by his closest working companion, "From this day forward, in order to hold my job, I no longer know your name."

The entire staff is encouraged to stay away from victims with the message that these people are on the way out. Fellow employees are thus intimidated and afraid to associate with the victims.

Signature Pattern No. 6: Numbing

(Nullifying Emotions And Ethics)

Kindness

Like spiders who numb their prey before the kill, Dragons are manipulators who spin a web of deception to gain trust before attacking their victims.

Bud, a middle-level manager for a southeastern manufacturing company, was unaware that he was marked for Dragon food. He knew, however, that his experience and credentials exceeded those of his bosses. Having been treated rudely from time to time by his supervisors throughout the past year (strategically spaced out to create confusion), Bud denied his anger, felt confused, and dreaded the upcoming annual evaluation interview. Much to his relief, he was greeted cordially.

Harly and Peter stated that they were doing the evaluation together to provide a comfort level so that an honest, heart-to-heart process could take place. Little did Bud know that he was in the company of not one but two Doorkeepers. They started out by asking Bud to list some of the positive things that took place during the past year. Bud enthusiastically brought up several problems that he had solved involving production and personnel.

After thanking Bud for his candor, the Doorkeepers eyed each other in silence. Then they started in. They took turns berating Bud for not reporting production problems to them before solving the problems. These attacks were falsehoods. In fact, Bud had previously sent written memos to both bosses informing them of each step in handling the problems. He had received no acknowledgment from his jealous Doorkeeper supervisors or the Dragon General Manager.

They then attacked Bud for being too soft on employees and working with them to solve problems rather than punishing the personnel. Next, the Doorkeepers asserted that any problem in Bud's department must be a sign of his weakness as a manager. They

> called him a "dummy" among other names. Subsequently, Bud received a two-page letter vaguely describing his attitude problem and shortcomings. Within six months, he was threatened with termination.

It was not long before Bud began to accept the idea that he was uncreative and careless. He became an ideal automaton, following orders without conscience and without resistance.

Threats

The threat of coercion usually weakens or destroys resistance more effectively than coercion itself! For example, the threat to inflict pain can trigger fears that become more damaging and more intimidating than the physical sensation of the pain itself. In Bud's case, the threat of losing his job sometime in the future was enough to numb his desire to resist the brainwashing that he was receiving.

Criticizing

Like all bullies, Dragons are good at attacking with threats but when they are threatened themselves, they become extremely defensive. They employ any means at hand to regain control of the situation.

Dragons are very astute at recognizing situations that call for different performances. They will turn on the charm and dodge the issue when embarrassed, caught in a lie, perceived as putting on a display of false emotion, or found to be ignorant of important information. The best defense is an overwhelming offense. In such circumstances, a typical Dragon will attack with an accusatory and punitive tone of voice the words, actions, and presumed motives of all who are daring to confront the Dragon.

That Doesn't Make Sense

This defensive counterattack is so common among these abusers that it is a signature pattern. The "that doesn't make sense" comment is designed to belittle and destroy victims and any who dare to come up with a rebuttal or confronting response. The following is but one example of how this remark is used.

> Ken, a railroad roadmaster (supervisor of track and station maintenance) and a Dragon, would call in a private contractor to plow the snow from the station platform instead of using the railroad maintenance staff. When Ken did this, the cost of plowing was charged against the operating department instead of the maintenance department. This trick made the maintenance department look financially efficient at the general headquarters. In reality, it was costing the company additional money because the maintenance workers were on duty and could have plowed the platforms at no extra cost. It made the operating department look less cost efficient.
>
> The Trainmaster in charge of the subdivision tried to explain to both the division headquarters and Ken what was happening and how it increased expenses for the company as a whole. Ken screamed at the Trainmaster, "That doesn't make sense," and went on with a threat that he had better not bring the subject up again, and he was stupid for even investigating the situation, and the conversation was over for good! Meanwhile the general and division headquarters, which were driven by data only, reprimanded the Trainmaster for not being a team player with Ken, the Roadmaster and Dragon.

There is an interesting side note to this example. The Division Superintendent was also a Dragon and supported the

Roadmaster. The Trainmaster was then designated for victimization with increased responsibilities because he had demonstrated a higher level of knowledge than the Dragon.

Placing the victim on the defensive and in an embarrassing position allows Dragons to evade any topic that would threaten their total control. They are off the hook, still retain power, and the victims are where they should be – walking on eggshells with the numbing process sapping their ability to resist.

The longer the abuser remains secure within a workplace and plays manipulative games as if they were simply victimless entertainment, the greater the damage done. Anyone within reach of the Dragon's influence either leaves immediately or becomes numb to moral principles, ethics, values, and social conscience. The victims deteriorate in these ways through denial and apathy. As abuses continue, the desire to fight back diminishes. Workers gradually lose their zeal, as well as their desire to be productive, create new ideas, and work for the good of the organization.

This numbing process happens so gradually that it is not until some victims show symptoms of profound anxiety and depression that they become aware of the seriousness of their predicament. Those with a good support system will recover, move on, and build new careers. Those who feel trapped under stressful conditions with little or no support are in danger of emotional and physical complications. (See Step III for more about feelings and stress.)

Summary

Abuses can be identified and tracked by the signature patterns of predatory behavior. The six most common Dragon tracks can be recalled by using the acronym D R A G O N as follows:

1. **Deception**

   This includes misleading, lying, dividing loyalties, creating disruption and chaos, promoting an imbalance of power, and moving to take over total control through intimidating, manipulating, and abusing power.

2. **Relationships**

   A predatory hierarchy is established with a clear pecking order reflecting on privilege, power, absolute control, and intimidation. Lower-level victims are typically tormented, abused, and devoured simply for the enjoyment of all those who agree to remain willing victims of the Dragon without complaint as a trade-off for some promised reward.

3. **Assessment**

   Dragons test candidates for Doorkeeper and victim status in their predatory hierarchies. The four-part scoring separates those victims who can be easily controlled and silenced from those who refuse to do so. Those who fail are unknowingly designated as Dragon food, to be nibbled on, abused, and tossed out either as fast food or as a banquet for others to intimidate and abuse before being fired.

4. **Grooming**

   The process used by all predators to develop pseudo-trust before victimizing. The three stages of victimization are grooming, the setup, and the hook. Anger serves as a natural warning system to protect one during the first two stages, but terror replaces anger once victims are hooked.

5. **Ostracizing**

   Predators isolate their victims to exert total control. Dragons in the workplace use ostracizing in a variety of forms to control their prey through social pressure while providing an intimidating warning to their other victims.

6. **Numbing**

   This is the process of brainwashing victims to ignore their own ethics, feelings, thoughts, and beliefs. They question their own misgivings, blame themselves for their own victimization, and attribute unwarranted power and allegiance to their abuser. Numbing ends resistance and makes victimization, as well as total control by the Dragon, possible.

Dragon-Tracking Checklist 3-1

Now that you are aware of the problems and characteristics of Dragons, use this list to determine whether or not there is a Dragon in your life.

Signature Patterns:

No. 1 *Deception*: Lies and Chaos
Examples:

No. 2 *Relationships*: Symbiotic and Abusive
Examples:

No. 3 *Assessment*: The Test
Examples:

No. 4 *Grooming*: Victimization and Recruiting
Examples:

No. 5 *Ostracizing*: Exclusion and Isolation
Examples:

No. 6 *Numbing*: Nullifying Emotions and Ethics
Examples:

Chapter 4

Power Games Dragons Play

Abusers enjoy using their power. They play a series of fairly identifiable, cruel, and sadistic games to dehumanize, pressure, and control their selected victims. Although there are many such games, we have chosen to unveil six of the most common ones for you. Dragons have their favorites that they repetitiously use in various situations; they are not really that creative. They tend to be rigid, so once you spot the games, you will find many variations of the same games repeated for you. You may wish to list your own Dragon's games in your Dragon diary as you spot them.

Dragons and Doorkeepers play these games according to specific unwritten rules which the victims are supposed to know without ever being told. Then Dragons congratulate themselves as their tortured victims lose dignity, self-esteem, security, and confidence. The abusers feel as though they have won another game.

When you learn to identify the *games* and realize that the Dragon's enjoyment is derived from your pain and confusion, you will be in a good place to resist reacting to provocation. Soon, you will be able to defend yourself. You will learn more about how to do this in Step IV, but for now, simply note the incidents in your Dragon diary (DD) as you discover them.

Game No. 1: Blind Man's Bluff (Keep 'Em in the Dark)

In this game, the Dragon withholds information so that the victim cannot effectively complete assignments. The lower-quality performance is then used for intimidating the employee. This game is a favorite because it assures the boss a winning hand.

One example that was brought to our attention took place at a university. During the spring semester of each year, a faculty review process awarded merits or demerits as reflected in pay scales for the upcoming contract year.

> The Dean (a Dragon) realized that Mark, the newest non-tenured professor, had credentials, a publishing record, and performances that far exceeded her own. She simply excluded Mark from all information relative to the process and sent the victim away from the campus on an assignment during the crucial evaluation time. Since the victim was not in attendance at the evaluation meeting, none of his credentials were introduced.
>
> Months later, when Mark received his new contract, he questioned the Dragon about the process. Mark was berated for numerous failures, including missing the evaluation meeting. She told him, "You have failed to live up to our expectations. You display many questionable professional characteristics that would support our low evaluation of your performance this year. You failed to submit complete documentation of your research and publishing activities in a timely manner prior to the meeting. You failed to list your professional accomplishments in detail and present them orally to the faculty. Your inadequacy in planning ahead is underscored by your being off campus during the evaluation process. By not participating in peer evaluation for the department, you have chosen to exclude yourself from all merit pay, promotions, and awards for the forthcoming year."

Mark received not only the wrath of the Dragon but a wage decrease equal to the Dragon's increase. She was congratulated for balancing the department's budget for another year. The victim immediately began a job search.

Dragons have been known to berate victims for not responding to previously sent directives. However, the memo was never dictated until the day after the berating and simply backdated in order to provide a paper trail to negatively affect the employee's file. *Manipulating information keeps the victim in the dark and the Dragon in control!*

Game No. 2: Divide and Conquer

In this game, the Dragon works to divide alliances or perceived alliances among staff by dropping bits of information or misinformation to first one person then the other. The system of dividing loyalties and friendships is done in a slick five-step process:

1. The Setup

The Dragon wishes to pit Jon (victim no. 1) against Oscar (victim no. 2). She begins by pointing out to Jon character flaws about him that were relayed to her in confidence by Oscar. However, such a conversation with Oscar never took place.

2. I'm on Your Side

The Dragon then discloses that the information came from Oscar and that she has chosen to give such information to Jon in order to "help you and your career."

3. Driving the Wedge

The manipulator then stands by to watch the results. Typically, Jon and Oscar quietly and gradually distance themselves from each other. In some cases, they might fight it out in the open.

4. Can You Keep Our Secret or Will You Keep Quiet and Protect Me?

If Jon discloses to Oscar that the information originated with the Dragon, he loses her support. If Jon protects the information source (the Dragon), then Jon and Oscar are divided. In either case, she has all the power and maintains control of both men.

5. Let's See the Two of You Fight or Do I Get to Punish You?

If either Jon or Oscar decides to argue openly, the Dragon gleefully punishes both parties and remains the powerful one. If Jon and Oscar choose to rise above these petty manipulations, a different outcome can occur. They may remain friends or calmly negotiate their differences. Such a move would threaten any Dragon. The punishment might be lateral transfers or demotions. In any case, the Dragon would drop them as candidates for power spots and immediately designate them as Dragon food.

An especially dangerous and costly form of the "divide and conquer" game is played within the business world when Dragons' unbridled competitiveness eats away at their own organizations. They actually take pleasure in recklessly defeating other departments without regard for the health of the companies or the welfare of the employees.

While giving lip service to cooperation, Dragons almost never enter into a mutual win-win effort for the good of the company. Thus, they deprive employees of their natural need for cooperation and respectful communication in the workplace. Furthermore, the divide and conquer game is played with departments as well as targeted victims. For example:

> At one mining facility, the competitive Dragons pitted each shift against the others. The "games" escalated to the point that each shift spent increasing amounts of valuable time hiding the appropriate tools from the next shift. Incoming shifts needed several hours to locate their tools before productive work could begin. Middle-management Dragons played this destructive game for years without detection. As production decreased, the company gradually declined and went out of business.

> A parts manufacturing company's Dragon CEO was quoted in private at an executive committee meeting as saying, "We do not want the departments working together. It takes away my power and gives it to the department heads. Our strategy will be to publicly encourage cooperative strategies but push the competition." As a result, when the marketing department called the production department to clarify a product specification, it was met with the response, "Why the hell do you want to know?"

Notice how the customers' and employees' needs got lost in the process. The Dragon is satisfied as long as blame can be shifted onto someone else.

Game No. 3: Heads I Win, Tails You Lose

(Double Bind, Bend the Mind)

Dragons continually place victims into a classic double bind. No matter which available option victims select, they are always wrong!

Example A

1. The Setup

   The Dragon orders the victim to do something.

2. Training the Dog

   The victim responds by doing exactly as told.

3. Brain Twisting

   The Dragon suddenly throws the victim off balance by asking, "Why did you do . . ." in a punishing tone of voice that implies, "Boy are you stupid for following my orders!"

The victim now has but three directions to go:

- Tell the truth
- Tell a lie
- Do not respond at all

If that person elects to tell the truth, "You ordered me to do it," the employee's statement implies that there is something wrong with the Dragon. Such statements are not permitted. Therefore, the victim is punished for being impudent. If the person elects to lie, "It was my own initiative," the victim is punished for not following orders explicitly. If the employee senses the double bind and decides not to answer, the victim is punished for being stupid.

Example B

1. The Setup

   The Dragon gives the victim a job to do.

2. Hands-off or You Choose

   The victim asks questions about how to do it. The Dragon remains "hands-off" by saying, "You can do it any way that you feel is best."

3. Brain Twisting

   The Dragon suddenly throws the victim off balance by asking in a punishing tone of voice, "Why did you use process XYZ?" The tone implies, "You better not question my question!"

If the victim says, "Permission was granted for me to make a choice," the reply will be, "You really made a stupid choice!" If the victim reminds the boss, "But I specifically asked for your assistance," the answer will be, "Don't try to lay the blame on me." The victim is caught in a double bind since nothing can be said that will satisfy a Dragon. Consequently, no matter which way the victim turns, the Dragon wins, and the predator's appetite has been satisfied for the moment.

In the drive to feed an insatiable appetite for power, a strange little scene ensues. The Dragon continues to use ploys that force victory after victory over increasingly helpless employees. Meanwhile, the employees are fighting for their emotional lives and for their careers. The health of the organization and the welfare of its customers get lost in the dynamics.

There are many cases in which these emotional struggles have cost companies dearly. For example:

> In one transportation company, an assistant vice president (AVP) for operations ordered Maria from the marketing-research staff to set up a meeting with a customer who formerly had been a regular shipper. Maria asked specifically what she should inquire about. The AVP responded, "There has been a sudden, significant decline in their shipments. Find out what the problem is and what we can do about it!" This counsel sounded straightforward. Maria contacted the shipper and then worked up a complete report for the Dragon on exactly what steps could be taken to recover the business.
>
> After reading the report, the AVP lashed out with a heads I win, tails you lose double bind. "Why the hell did you ask the shipper what our company can do about the problem?" And the AVP went on, "Now either we have to do what the shipper wants done or we will never get their business back. We have lost their business, and it is all your fault!"
>
> The AVP, who had caused the problem by downsizing, successfully blamed the research department, and no one suspected that he was a Dragon. Maria, sensing the dysfunctional workplace, began a job search. Secretarial staff members began to leave saying that the boss was impossible. Nobody listened. Unfor-

tunately, the company was permeated with Dragons and Doorkeepers. The company ultimately went bankrupt.

Game No. 4: Musical Chairs

Dragon activity within an organization usually depletes the talent pool by triggering the emigration of skilled, competent employees to other firms. Lost talent is seldom replaced. Instead, the company receives an influx of less experienced and more easily harassed replacements. Dragons create this talent-draining turnover rate while maintaining the appearance of doing a great management job.

In one situation, Mike replaced a departing marketing manager, a victim of a well-entrenched Dragon CEO, in a West Coast manufacturing company. Mike was recognized as a *"team player"* by the CEO and hired on the spot. Within three months, Mike had not only selected several staff members for Dragon food but had all of the marketing agents pitted against each other. Seven of the nine staff members quit. When the Board of Directors inquired of the President about the many turnovers, the response was, "They were against change."

A new group of people was hired. Out of the seven hired, four left within six months. When the Board again inquired, the CEO gave the same response, along with praise for Mike indicating what a superb job he had done for the department since he had come onboard. The CEO commented about the *stability* that Mike added to a *constantly changing environment.* (Notice the duality in the CEO's responses to his Board of Directors.) Sales figures were not available, but exit interviews cited extreme job stress as the common reason for employees departing, although nothing was ever done about it!

Fortunately for business, the majority of workers are psychologically healthy. Healthy people do not tolerate abuse. They begin to feel angry. They heed their warning signs. As certain new insiders advance toward Doorkeeper status, the healthy ones reject the grooming. They are often seen in the workout room or at the employee assistance counselor's office as they attempt to deal with the excessive stress created by what has become a dysfunctional work setting.

Game No. 5: Blame and Shame, That's Our Game

Dragons typically point the finger of blame and shame at others but never see the other three fingers of the hand pointing back at them. The function of the Dragon is to dish out blame and shame to others at all times.

> Susan, a RN at a health care facility, had been carefully selected for Dragon food. She eventually resigned because of the blame constantly leveled at her in the workplace. No matter what took place, Susan was blamed for it. If any patient's room had not been cleaned, even though Susan had nothing to do with the cleaning services, she was blamed for it.
>
> Sometimes mistakes would be made on the instruction sheets for patient care. Because of Susan's victim status, she would politely inquire about the set of instructions. Instead of an answer, the Dragon boss would go into a screaming fit and yell, "Don't blame me for the problem. If you knew better, you would know how to fix it." It was not Susan's job to change the doctor's orders, but the implication was always there. "If

you were not so stupid, you would know exactly what to do!"

This is a familiar game. Nearly everyone knows how to point the finger of blame, but blame is the lifeblood of Dragons who typically feel that they are in a unique position. Blame must point away from them.

Game No. 6: The Rumpelstiltskin Ploy

The employee review is a legitimate method of documenting supervisory contacts and typically includes a review of past and present job functioning and a plan for the future. The best reviews are about 40% review and 60% preview to encourage and motivate employees toward personal and company goals. Letters of reprimand are also legitimate to document problem areas and are typically positive in their inclusion of suggestions for improvement. They are written for the benefit of the employee as well as the company.

When an employee cannot meet written expectations, deficiencies are easily exposed with honest, legitimate supervision and documentation. There is no need for falsification of records, half-truths, pressuring, threatening, etc. Dragons, jealous of anyone who will not submit to their abuse, often use reprimands and memos as weapons. This technique is usually saved for the "Olympic athlete" of the victim population – the victim who is quite competent, has much support from other employees, customers, administrators, or the public, and who is difficult to subdue openly.

This process is called the "Rumpelstiltskin ploy," meaning that if you cannot do them in easily, then set them up by demanding that they spin straw into gold. The next step is to reprimand them for being slow while adding more tasks, more piles of straw. Then berate them for not meeting expectations, timelines, and so on until they resign. As a side note, when people ask a Dragon boss about how they can effectively accomplish the increased workload, a typical response is, "You are just going to have to do more with less. Everybody else is doing it!"

Discussion

Dragon tracking involves observing the signature patterns as well as the games carried out against individuals and groups over a period of time. One isolated event does not necessarily indicate a dysfunctional workplace. However, over a period of time, Dragon patterns and abusive *power games* signal the strong possibility of major problems within the workplace.

Exercise 1

Think about an incident in which you or someone else felt like a victim. Can you remember seeing any Dragon tracks or recognizing any Dragon games having been played?

Exercise 2

Using Checklist 3-1, Dragon Tracking (p. 51), score your observations to the following criteria:

- I have not seen — 1 point
- Once in awhile — 2 points
- This seems to be a pattern — 3 points

There are 18 total points possible. The higher the score, the greater the possibility that the organization is under the influence of a Dragon.

Exercise 3

Using Checklist 4-1, Game Spotting (p. 64), score your observations:

- None — 1 point
- Once in a while — 2 points
- A regular occurrence — 3 points

Again, the higher the score out of the 18 points possible, the greater the possibility that your boss is a Dragon.

Game Spotting Checklist 4-1
Games That I Have Observed

No. 1 *Blind Man's Bluff* (Keep 'Em in the Dark)
Examples:

No. 2 *Divide and Conquer*
Examples:

No. 3 *Heads I Win, Tails You Lose* (Double Bind)
Examples:

No. 4 *Musical Chairs*
Examples:

No. 5 *Blame and Shame, That's Our Game*
Examples:

No. 6 *The Rumpelstiltskin Ploy*
Examples:

Other Games That I Have Noticed or Suspect
Examples:

Step III

Honor Your Anger

Feelings are human. They are there to help you enjoy life. They serve as a natural, internal communication system that enables you to experience life to the fullest. One of the outcomes of being targeted by a Dragon boss is that you feel *anger*. Anger is perhaps one of the most important but least understood of all human feelings and can, in turn, lead to stress, distress, and depression.

Learn about, appreciate, and trust your anger, as it is the early alarm system that can protect you from victimization. Predators always begin their deception by attempting to disengage those natural feelings while subjecting their victims to pressures and stressful situations. Long before you know the reality of your situation, your feelings will lead you in the safest direction once your intellect learns to understand their special messages.

In this third step, we clarify the three stages of anger and how they relate to stress or distress in life. We then move on to nine other normal feelings that warn and protect you. We will give you ideas for handling stress and the anger traps that may lie in your way. Then we will show you methods for escaping those pitfalls while staying in control of your life. Once you understand your feelings, you can fight the confusing effects of being in a stressful workplace, gain control, and put your life back on track.

Chapter 5

Trust Your Anger Alarm

Do not fear your anger; it is your ally. Anger is a complex and often misunderstood emotion. It exists as an honorable feeling that can warn you of danger and give you the strength to fight injustice.

Anger acts as nature's alarm system. Victims feel it at each stage of the grooming process, as their bodies automatically prepare for the fight-or-flight process. Victims are systematically trained to ignore their internal, early warning system of angry feelings. At the last stage of victimization, when they are hooked, they feel only terror.

If you are angry, you are doing well. Your anger is not a problem, but what you do with your angry feelings may well become a problem. So let's take a fresh look at anger according to its levels of intensity.

First-Degree Anger

Although annoying, first-degree anger is hardly life threatening. It is that "ticked-off" type of anger that we feel when someone crosses our boundaries. It is what you feel when someone cuts ahead of you in the check-out line or your boss stands too close to you and violates your personal space. We learn to live and deal with these annoyances on a daily basis. In fact, most of us experience something that could trigger first-degree anger nearly every fifteen minutes.

We certainly could not be bothered by getting upset for every little affront that occurs, so we don't. We handle our responses to this anger alarm with our social skills. We communicate. Typically we count to ten, cool down, speak up if necessary, then simply let go of the incident and resume our everyday lives. Normal people do not brood, hang on to insults, or deliberately provoke violence in response to first-degree anger.

Second-Degree Anger

Anger in the second degree is more than just a temporary annoyance; it recurs. The emotional pain keeps gaining our attention. The angry feeling is a signal, an alarm that sends out a warning to your entire body. Just like a smoke alarm that warns you of danger, your anger says to you, "Look for the problem! Look for the problem! Check to see if you're in danger!"

For example, your boss shouts at you, but you are too shocked to answer. The verbal abuse continues. You respond respectfully, but your heart is racing. You calm yourself down and return to work intending to do your best, but the words ring in your memory. You feel distracted, fearful, and confused about what happened. You feel angry at having been disturbed by such unpleasant feelings. It seems unfair. The next time that the boss is near as you are working, your heart races, and you feel angry, tense, and distracted. Your angry "*it's not fair*" feelings recur.

Do not ignore the alarm. Do some serious problem identification. Look for options and decide what changes are possible for you. Then take action. If you feel confused, discuss your feelings with someone who can help to give you direction. Most of us can handle second-degree anger problems alone, but the complex ones typically call for consultation. The point is, take care of problems when they are small. Do not wait until you are furious, explosive, and well into third-degree anger.

Third-Degree Anger

Third-degree anger could indicate that your life is in danger.

> Whenever I see my boss, I feel my blood pressure rising. I have fantasies of being powerful enough to fire him. I feel myself being preoccupied with ways to sidestep his abuses. It's interfering with my work. I'm afraid I will make a mistake. In my field, that could cost someone's

> life. I don't sleep well at night, and I find myself getting angry for no reason at all. I feel trapped, blocked, and I'm losing self-confidence. I fear for the future. The stress is getting to me. I'll be seeing the doctor next week.

The emotional pain of third-degree anger does not subside until the problem causing the alarm is addressed and solved. Anger of this magnitude often precedes severe symptoms of physical and psychological distress leading to health problems and may be a precursor to violence, murder, or suicide. Anger at this level lets us know that time is running out. Painful symptoms such as preoccupation with violence, depression, sleeplessness, and agitation chip away at one's ability to locate the problem, evaluate alternatives, make realistic decisions, and move on in life. Third-degree anger calls for major changes. Blocked anger of such intensity can require therapeutic solutions.

What Is Your Anger Telling You?

First-Degree Anger

I can tolerate the emotional pain. I realize that the company is dysfunctional, but I feel healthy enough to put that aside and still be proud of the work that I do. I can take my time before making concrete changes in one direction or another.

Second-Degree Anger

It's getting to me. I find myself getting angrier each day. It is affecting other aspects of my life. The stress is taking its toll on my self-respect. I am beginning to lose confidence, and I am not enjoying my work anymore. I must begin to assess my alternatives and move toward making some changes. I cannot seem to kick the anger that I feel, no matter what I do and how I change. I feel as though I am spinning my wheels.

Third-Degree Anger

I am finding myself preoccupied with the workplace situation. I feel intense hatred toward my boss and wish I could carry out some sort of revenge. I find myself wishing my boss were dead. I feel pained enough to imagine myself dead. I obsess over alternatives and have done everything I can on the job to resolve the problems. I still feel as though I am getting nowhere. I know I must make changes in my job and my life, and I must make them soon.

So How Angry Are You?

My anger level is in the:

First Degree: My anger is mild but tolerable. It's warning me of possible abuses in my workplace.

Second Degree: My recurring anger is annoying and distracting. I need to pay attention to a problem and see what I can do to take care of it.

Third Degree: My obsession and preoccupation with thoughts about retaliation, depression, homicide, or suicide are intolerable. These types of feelings are very serious, and they demand immediate attention, problem identification, problem resolution, and change.

Are Your Ready to Explode?

Do any of these thoughts seem familiar to you?

- What about violence? No matter what I do, it seems that I have no choice but an attack. I have tried everything else, and nothing changes – bullies never change. I would like to attack the boss, but I know I can't. It would do no good.
- I am so angry that I fantasize about getting revenge, and it scares me.
- Sometimes I have an urge to kill. I know I would not really do it, but what are the chances that I could?

Relax! It is normal that extreme fantasies come into play when people are desperately searching for options in seemingly impossible situations. Rarely do these fantasies become reality. Those who have had previous mental or anger-control problems and those who abuse alcohol or drugs are, however, at high risk for becoming violent. No matter how victimized you feel, violence is never the answer. It only creates more problems.

Fantasizing about violence (a third-degree anger warning) calls for immediate outside help. ***Do not*** *try to handle such problems alone. Long-term, high-intensity stress takes its toll in terms of your physical and mental health.*

Do You Feel Angry, Resentful, and Irritated?

Those feelings that we typically acknowledge as anger can be thought of as a smoke screen for a confusing array of underlying feelings. To solve an anger problem, you must deal with those feelings that are just beneath the anger as well as the problem that is triggering the anger alarm.

The most frequent feeling hiding under anger is fear. If you are puzzled by someone's anger, just hypothesize that they are afraid, and you will be right most of the time. If you are puzzled by your own anger, ask yourself, "What is it that I fear the most?"

Often, people fear:

- Someone's power
- Change
- Emotional pain
- Physical pain
- Injury
- Retaliation
- Punishment
- The future
- Abuse

The second most frequent feeling found behind a screen of anger is loss. People may feel they have lost:

- Face
- Power
- Career
- Position
- Opportunity
- Health
- Money, property, or material goods
- Love, affection, intimacy, sex
- Status
- Credibility
- Life

The third most frequent feeling beneath anger is betrayal. People may feel betrayed by:

- Unfair treatment
- Humiliation caused by a former loved one or friend
- Mistrust
- Being cheated
- Being abused
- Being victimized
- Being misled
- Being defamed
- Legal maneuvers

When you are dealing with a Dragon, you may be feeling a mixture of all of the above emotions. This mix of emotions is why the situation is so confusing and so difficult to handle alone.

Anger is your first defense against being victimized. Your feeling of anger alerts you to the presence of a Dragon. It sends an emotionally alerting message long before you are ready to cut through your denial and recognize a setup for victimization. Like any warning system, however, there are smart things you can do in response to the signal, and there are less intelligent things you can do. For example, when your smoke detector goes off in the middle of the night, some of the foolish things you could do are:

- Take the batteries out to stop the noise and then go back to sleep.
- Dance around the room to the music of the beep, beep, beep.
- Put a pillow over your head to deaden the sound and filter the smoke.

Among the smarter things you could do are:

- Get up, search for the cause of the alarm.
- Grab a flashlight, look for smoke, and be ready to evacuate.
- Evacuate and then dial 911.

There are smart things and there are foolish things you can do when your anger alarm is sounding. Among the foolish things you could do are:

- Ignore your feelings then go home from work and kick the dog.
- Deny your anger and ignore the problems until "job stress" gets you down.
- Break a window or sabotage some tools.
- Punch the boss in the nose.

The smarter things you could do are:

- Honor your anger and heed its warning by checking out the problems.
- Document, document, document.
- Decide if your problem can be handled alone or whether you need assistance to speak out on your own behalf.
- Consider your alternatives and then act.

Your anger is your friend; acknowledge it; appreciate it. Pay attention to it and congratulate yourself on your perceptiveness.

Then, you can focus on the stress and the other feelings underlying anger as you make your way toward taking charge of your future.

Stress and Emotions

Emotions are labels we use to identify different sorts of stress. But first, we will examine stress itself. Stress is the term most of us use when we feel pressure and are confused about our body states, mixed feelings, and our thoughts. However, life has both positive and negative stresses. Positive stress is doing something that we like to do, and it takes quite a bit of energy to do it. Examples of this stress include running a 100-yard dash in a track meet or cooking a complex meal for your future spouse who is coming over for dinner. Negative stress, on the other hand, can be caused by long hours on the job, especially when you have been targeted for constructive dismissal and do not yet know it.

Negative stress can have effects on the brain and the body. Negative stress seems to deplete B vitamins, proteins, trace minerals, energy sources, and our immune system. So what can we do? We can use our intelligence to secure appropriate nutrition along with adequate rest and exercise. Of course, what you eat, which hormones are available, how capable your body is to circulate its blood (and hormones), and how efficiently your brain's energy-supply system functions all make a difference in how well your brain can achieve its potential.

Humans have a unique intellect. We have imagination, beliefs, and feelings. We are creative and can perceive abstract ideas. We can put many concepts together to plan ahead. We have free will. We make judgments, solve problems, anticipate consequences, and can change negative stress into positive action. We can demand our legitimate rights and needs even if we are perceived as being obnoxious. We can delay gratification at will.

We humans can sabotage abusive attempts to inflict emotional pain on us simply by seeing such acts as humorous or ridiculous. We can decide whether or not to take another's provocation seriously. We can laugh. We can use our incredible human mind to handle our distress by understanding it and then taking decisive action.

Humans are not perfect. One of the imperfections we as therapists witness involves the rather intricate but clumsy way individuals handle stress. When negative stress occurs, our primitive alarm system engages without assistance from our intellect. However, we humans need that higher-order mental function to identify, direct, and control stress.

The body prepares for stress through what Hans Selye described as the General Adaptation Syndrome (GAS). In this mechanism, symptoms (such as raised adrenaline, increased heart rate, influx of oxygen from the lungs, slow digestion, and blood flowing to the muscles) result from rising stress. However, until the higher-order areas of the brain recover enough blood flow to focus and identify the stress, neurons seem to hesitate.

For example, you may be startled by a voice in the dark and begin to shake until you see a loved one and recognize a familiar laugh. The instant your mind lets you know that you are safe, calming hormones take over, and you may feel pleasant stress in anticipation of togetherness and companionship.

It is the GAS that sends the body into a state of emergency. But it is the incredible human intellect that labels the emergency as exciting, thrilling, or dangerous and helps one focus energy in a particular direction.

The stress that debilitates humans is *distress.* We usually feel distressed when our thoughts, feelings, intellect, needs, and emotions collide simultaneously. Like a child's battery-powered locomotive that is stuck spinning its wheels out of control until its batteries run down, our neurons appear to fire and thoughts vacillate back and forth in a disorganized fashion. Because of the constant adrenaline flow and other biochemical consequences of nature's alarm system, we are unable to think clearly about the problem and appear to be blocked from taking action toward resolving it. At such time, we can become emotionally depleted, suffer increased illness, and show symptoms of clinical depression or physical deterioration.

The antidote for *distress* is not war on stress, denial, attack, getting even, or any of a number of other misguided actions. It is *focusing* your stress, recognizing your feelings and your options, and then using your personal power to change things. However, do pay attention to the pitfalls or traps on the road to change.

Anger Traps

Anger is not a problem. How you display your anger may become one. However well justified you may feel in venting rage toward your oppressor, it seldom does anything toward changing the situation, problem solving, or relieving your negative stress. Mismanaged anger entraps its own victim by enhancing a Dragon's status while undermining the victim's.

Trap No. 1: Clowning

Often people who struggle with the negative attention of an abusive boss resort to clowning. Such blatant attempts to hide from the truth or push the stress out of mind seldom work. The victims say to themselves, "If I laugh about it, I won't cry," or "Perhaps it (the stress, the abuse, the anger) will go away." The victim is only denying the seriousness of the problem and is making a big mistake.

> Bill, who was slated for Dragon food, was a traffic marketing/sales representative for a trucking firm. He responded to his negative stress by clowning around, joking with customers, and ridiculing the boss behind his back. In his effort to avoid the problem, keep up a happy front, and survive each day, he unwittingly walked right into a trap. When word got back to the boss that

> Bill was not taking his work seriously, he had provided the boss with a legitimate reprimand for his file. The problem was compounded by Bill's behind-the-back comments regarding the boss. The Dragon then had a legitimate excuse to terminate Bill.

It may seem as though "whistling in the dark" would prevent fear and depression and thus provide some security if even for just a short time. This is not true. The anger and stress that accompany a Dragon attack are there with or without the funny business. Such clowning simply allows the Dragon and Doorkeepers to point out to others that you are inane or silly and not to be taken seriously. When you have a serious problem, you need to confront it as such. Your feelings warn you that something needs to be done.

Trap No. 2: Addictions

Some people stop at the bar after work or use drugs to deal with their painful emotions. Using such substances for their effect on one's mood is a prime cause of serious addictive disorder. The social drinker, for example, may have a drink or two in a social situation but never for the effect of the drug. However, the alcoholic drinks for the drugging effect of the alcohol: dulling the mind, allowing one to forget, and quieting the feelings of failure for a time.

In a drugged state, some people report a feeling of pseudo-confidence, while others simply sink deeper into depression. Temporary relief sought by altering the brain chemistry is never worth the price of experimenting with addictive substances. It is far better to face reality and deal with your problems than to add a multitude of new problems to your life.

Trap No. 3: Affairs

Finding themselves increasingly isolated at work and overwhelmed with discouragement, many victims have difficulty sharing the depth of their despair with their loved ones. They may look to a stranger or a new friend to share an intimate moment. Watch out! A one-night stand, an exciting person for an evening, is a charming trap!

Those who deal with diminishing self-confidence through extramarital affairs have pulled away from loved ones. Rather than share their fears of failure with a spouse and risk being misunderstood, they often stop engaging their loved ones in intimate and loving communication. With poor communication at home, they may feel motivated to take a chance on a new love. In acting out a fantasy, they hope to gain a sense of well-being or a temporary sense of relief from their problems by connecting with someone new. Such solutions are shortsighted as well as short-lived because future problems are sure to multiply. Along with facing Dragon attacks, the victims face serious marital problems while their loved ones become secondary victims of the Dragon.

Trap No. 4: Gambling

It is hard to resist the lure of money as a cure-all for financial worries when job security is uncertain. Gambling and the dream of unimaginable wealth may entice the social gambler to venture deeply into debt. Unfortunately, the thought of a big win as a solution to all troubles is a foolish dream. The odds are always against it. Gamblers lose more money than they win. Furthermore, the targeted victim who gambles on a win instead of dealing with reality becomes more dependent on the Dragon-controlled job than before. Gambling debt becomes a sinkhole, which insures that the Dragon will have continued subservience from the victim.

Trap No. 5: Retaliating

Some victims try to bolster their sagging self-confidence by getting even, back-biting, or sabotaging the workplace. Such misguided acts tend to boomerang. As soon as the victim is spotted as the perpetrator of annoying pranks, he or she is judged to be the villain. Thus, the Dragon is again seen as blameless while the victim falls into the trap of providing evidence for a justified dismissal.

Trap No. 6: Abusing Others

Abusing others, becoming Dragon-like yourself, is never a solution to working with a Dragon. Remember, they are power drunk. They want to rob you of your personal power, place you in the position of a victim, and destroy you. But you have the ability to cope with a Dragon while making plans to move forward. (See Step IV.)

So in order to avoid the traps, what can a person do when in a situation where anger levels are rising? There are several things that a person should do and some that one should not do. For example:

- *Do Not Attack*

  Stifle that urge to kill. Telling off the boss or counter attacking is one of the worst moves that you can make.

- *Do Not Defend Yourself*

  Putting others on the defensive is food for the Dragon. All you get from defensiveness is more Dragon breath. When the Dragon is raging and you are not defending, you are in power. Preserve your own dignity and refuse to stoop to attacking the dignity of the abuser. Eventually, it should become obvious to the organization that the system is in trouble, but that does not always happen.

- *Do Not Cower*

  Dragons feel more powerful when you grovel. Their attacks increase in proportion to the degree those about them fall apart. These predators have no power when you and others refuse to cower.

- *Do Look the Dragon in the Eye*

  Dragons expect victims to lower their eyes and cower. They are uncomfortable when people look them directly in the eye, especially when these people are designated victims. Keep your dignity and address the Dragon with your eyes.

- *Do Sidestep the Dragon's Breath*

  When the Dragon is breathing down your neck with flaming words, use a poker face. Control the urge to roll your eyes in disgust. Be careful not to smile – this might betray your secret pleasure in maintaining dignity. The abuser suffers when you do not respond as expected to an attack

- *Do Let the Dragon Rage*

  The Dragon expects you to defend yourself. Avoid this trap. Allow the raging to continue but silently concentrate on the facts that give you a chance to focus your efforts.

- *Do Sidestep the Personal Attacks and Change Topics*

  Acknowledge the Dragon's position and then change the topic to a neutral one or a business concern. For example:

  Boss: "You %&# lamebrain! What the hell is wrong with you? I don't care about your idiotic ideas. No one told you to change anything. Now keep your mouth shut and do as you are told around here or you'll be on the unemployment line next month with the rest of the deadbeats!"

  You: "I hear you, boss. What is it about the changes that you see as unworkable? How do you want the ABC situation handled?"

- *Do Understand What the Dragon Expects*

  Whether the Dragon is loud and abusive or the quiet, passive-aggressive type, all Dragons expect to stay in power through intimidation, fear, and punishment tactics. They are masters at the art of using your own anger to trap and defeat you. They expect to manipulate you until you lose control. Most of us cannot think well or react with decorum when the adrenaline is rushing through us. They expect you to be afraid, cower, defend yourself, and respond in an "angry" counterattack. If you do so, the boss looks good, and you look bad. Dragons are rigid. When victims do not respond predictably, they become confused and are thrown off course.

Summary

Anger as a protective alarm requires understanding and different responses according to the level of threat one experiences. It is a secondary response to a primary threat or hurt. Like a smoke detector, it is a very important early warning that potential victims need to acknowledge. Even when anger is numbed by grooming, it may be felt as distress as it continues to send out the warning that there is an important threat for you to deal with - *now*. The anger is not the problem, but how to interpret its message and what you do with the anger may very well be problematic issues for you. Be aware of the anger traps and learn how to escape them. Learn how to handle stress while decreasing the amount of distress in your life.

Questions

1. Think about the last time you experienced anger in the workplace. Did you fall into any of the anger traps mentioned in this chapter? If so, which ones, and what were the results?
2. What are some of the positive stresses in your life?
3. What is one distressing situation that you have encountered during the last year, and how are handling your feelings regarding this situation?
4. What steps have you taken toward resolving the distressing problem?

Chapter 6

Deal with Depression

You Are Not Alone

In addition to anger, the protective emotion, there are other perfectly normal but often confusing feelings that arise when you are working in a dysfunctional setting. Here are samples of some of the most intimate feelings expressed in the privacy of the therapeutic setting by a variety of workplace victims prior to therapy. Have you had similar thoughts and feelings?

- I'm really ticked - no angry - no outraged! The problem is my boss, but it could be me.
- The stress is getting to me. Maybe it's burnout. Whatever- I'm not sure about anything!
- Confused! That's it! I can't seem to think clearly. No matter what I do, no matter what move I make, I always lose ground. I think I'm thinking clearly, but when the boss is around, I feel like a loser. It was never like this before. Could I be at risk for Alzheimer's?
- I feel victimized, but I cannot remember being bullied. I have no bruises, but I feel like I've been beaten up. Nothing I do now is okay, and I don't understand why. My boss is on my back all the time. I cannot think at work.
- I feel powerless. My life is out of control, and my job is on the line.
- I'm slipping intellectually. The boss keeps threatening me. I'm working as hard as I can, but I cannot keep up with the demands no matter how I try. Could this lead to actual violence?
- Simple, everyday decisions are getting tougher each day - like to get out of bed and go to work.
- My friends are abandoning me. Or is it that I am withdrawing from them? I'm not sure at this point, but I really feel alone.

- I got the assignment, but I still hear those words in my head, "Here's your last chance, but you'll never make it. You and I both know that you're on your way out."
- I feel so down. I've lost my old spark. I feel tired – too tired to fight anymore.
- I'm constantly blaming myself for what I realize are normal human errors, no matter who makes them. I beat myself up for little things that I formerly considered simple hurdles to be handled easily and dismissed.
- The more hours I put in on the job, the more new assignments and pressures are added to my original workload. Nothing I've done this year was included in my job performance ratings.
- If I didn't know better, I would believe that my evaluations were biased in favor of the boss's prediction that I'd fail. How could that be? There are two other evaluators on the job. They are, or at least they were, my buddies. We all felt part of the group-close to the boss. We got all the inside information about what was really going on in the shop. That was before I began to pick up that I was a black sheep. All I did was ask a question. I guess it was the wrong one. I'm getting nervous. Mixed up – alone – stressed. Yes, that's it. I'm stressed!
- My career has me so worried that it's giving me trouble at home. My wife asked me if I was having an affair! I'm so upset about work, can't sleep, can't eat, making love is the last thing on my mind these days. I need help – no, not scared – terrified!
- I'm so down that I've actually been vacillating back and forth between thoughts of murdering my boss and suicide. I know I wouldn't really do either, my church – you know – but I wish I were dead. That really worries me!
- Blind alleys...I'm blocked. I feel like punching somebody. I know I can't. It would be the end of my job. I know that some of the answers I get are clearly misinformation and have led me into blind alleys, sapping my time. I don't know who's behind it. Sometimes I feel like I'm missing a big piece of the puzzle.

I'm so mad, but I don't know at whom to be angry. It really gets to a guy.

Notice how very few of the above statements reveal that the individuals knew that they were depressed. The victim often misses the signs of reactive states of depression, which seem to jump out to the professional. Once groomed and hooked, victims are typically in denial. They easily identify with the anger, the stress, and the confusion, but the most difficult emotions are the ones that are shame based. For example, some people feel guilt in having been hooked, deceived, or betrayed. For others, it is the shame of having compromised one's values and having been victimized that makes the emotions particularly difficult to face. Many people feel disappointed, as well as grief-stricken and remorseful, when what they thought was a fabulous career opportunity turns out to be Dragon smoke, and they are faced with multiple losses plus unforeseen career changes.

Now, What About You? Self-Study Checklist 6-1

As you look through the following list, circle the feelings with which you currently identify. Read on for information about depression and how it can impact your emotional well-being.

	A	B	C
1.	Angry	Tense	Happy
2.	Mystified	Confused	Thinking clearly
3.	Blaming	Obsessed	Relaxed
4.	Powerless	Confident	Powerful
5.	Fearful	Self-doubting	Worried but confident
6.	Outraged	Blocked	Determined
7.	Unable to plan	Future-oriented	Under control with goals
8.	Depressed	Disappointed	Realistic
9.	Suicidal	Seeking answers	Contemplating change
10.	Violent	Rational	Understanding feelings

Victimized people typically circle many feelings in column A. As they acquire insight and become less confused, they progress through columns B and C. Those who are able to get their lives back under control and move ahead in their careers, despite having had to deal with a Dragon and a dysfunctional workplace, typically circle many of the feelings in column C.

Depression

It is natural to feel sad, discouraged, and disappointed when your career plans are upset. Such feelings are usually replaced with more positive ones, like those in column C above, when insight or "movement" occurs, and the problems are identified. The secret to handling blocked anger is to focus that anger energy on the problems that block you. You are doing just that by reading this book. You are also getting a head start on dealing with your problems by writing in your DD and preparing for change. In the meantime, if some of your feelings are listed in column A, you might find the following suggestions helpful in working with your everyday emotional lows.

1. When you feel like staying in bed instead of going to work, get up. Increase your physical activity, and the urge to withdraw usually stops. Body movement increases the circulation of those hormones that chase away the blues and increases those that give your brain a lift. Exercise, walk, jog, or run.
2. If your low times at work leave you with a fantasy of physically punching your Dragon in the nose, you might try Monique's strategy of increasing physical activity while pretending to beat up her boss.

> Monique secured an early morning part-time job as a custodian where, with each stroke of her mop, she gleefully swatted the Dragon's face that she visualized on the wet floor. She

dealt with her frustration, finished her chores in record time, and was able to go home for a refreshing nap before work. Not only did it raise her spirits and her tolerance level, she also earned extra cash and became more physically fit in the process.

3. If you have no appetite, make each meal small but nourishing. Take the time to meet with a friend for a snack. Sometimes just the conversation is far more valuable than the food itself.

4. If you are feeling lonely, gather together a few of your coworkers and start you own support group. Talking about your feelings and your pressures with others who share the same workplace can help all of you through the tough times. For guidelines in using this book as a study guide, see Appendix I.

Those who are spinning their wheels or stuck in third-degree anger could sink into debilitating depression. Along with feelings of helplessness and hopelessness, it seems impossible for them to be assertive about their needs. Because victimization is often so mystifying, many people do not realize that they are actually depressed. If anyone you know is showing signs of blocked anger and a depressed state, reach out to them. Talk with them. Be a sounding board. Be a helping hand but never betray their confidence.

Could you be depressed? Learn more about it by using the following informal checklist of questions that may signal a generalized state of depression.

Blocked Anger and Depression Checklist 6-2

1. Do you find yourself avoiding experiences that you once enjoyed?
2. Are you having trouble getting enough sleep?
3. Do you feel too intimidated to face the Dragon or respond to criticism on the job?
4. Have you noticed being ill more often than usual?
5. Have you wondered to yourself, "How can I go on with my life?"
6. Do you try to hide your sadness from others to protect them?
7. Are you ashamed of being afraid or sad?
8. Do you think that if you admit how depressed you are that you will be considered weird, a wimp, crazy, unmanly, etc.?
9. Are you indecisive?

Other forms of depression are very severe and can last from a few weeks to several years. Severe depression calls for professional intervention and, at times, medication. Untreated depression can take its toll in terms of your physical health as well as your social relations and can, in some cases, lead to death. If you still have doubts about the severity of your depression and whether or not you should seek out a professional opinion, check out the questions in the following list.

Degree of Depression Checklist 6-3

- During the past few months, have you lost or gained more than 5% of your body weight per month without trying?
- Do you feel worthless or guilty without any basis?
- Do you have trouble sleeping, or do you sleep too much?
- Do you feel a loss of energy?
- Do you feel sad and empty most of the day, nearly every day?
- Do you have markedly diminished interest or pleasure in nearly all activities most of the day, nearly every day?
- Has your lack of interest or enthusiasm been noticed by others?
- Has anyone mentioned that you are too restless or too lethargic?
- Are you indecisive?
- Do you have recurring thoughts of death or suicidal ideation without a plan?
- Have you seriously thought about suicide and made a plan?

According to the American Psychiatric Association's DSM-IV, Diagnostic and Statistical Manual of Mental Disorders, answering "yes" to more than half of the above questions may indicate a Major Depressive Episode. Just as in any health-related issue, however, self-diagnosis can be dangerous. Be wise. Fight denial by facing the truth. Seek the opinion of a professional counselor, therapist, or physician if you or the friend you're helping seems to be showing signs of clinical depression and may be in need of assistance.

Chapter 7

Handling Stress

Have you noticed how you can spend many hours involved in stressful work that you enjoy? Time seems to pass quickly, yet you continue to feel energized and involved. Your body may feel tired but you sleep well at night, arising with renewed energy and eagerness to return. You feel good about yourself, and the stress is positive.

However, fifteen minutes spent on a task when you are feeling victimized, angry, or unduly pressured – one that depletes your self-esteem – feels like hours. You are exhausted, but your mind will not let you sleep peacefully because it races to make sense of the negative stress from which you seek relief.

It is this negative stress that sends the nervous system and physical reserves into panic. For example, during a profound anger episode, where you feel totally enraged and "lose it," your heart can beat twice as fast and blood pressure can rise to double or triple its usual rate. For the marathon runner or the well-trained athlete, these changes do not cause a problem. If you are out of shape or prone to artery or heart disease, the danger period for heart attack or stroke ranges from about six to twenty-four hours following an intense episode of negative stress. Any healthy person can withstand short periods of such stress. It is the long-term stress and the extreme feelings of distress that take their toll. Using your human intellect to understand what is happening and then focusing your stress enables neurons to return the system to its normal functioning. That is when you feel in control once again.

Stress is one of the best motivators toward making positive changes in your life. Turning from distress to focusing your energy on overcoming adversity is no miracle or magic act. It is not genetic; it is learned, and you can learn to do it, too! Here's how:

Attitude

Basically, it is not what happens to you but your perception of what is happening that determines what is positive or negative stress. The most important gains in life typically involve challenges, overcoming obstacles, learning, growing, experiencing the thrill of mastering new concepts or new skills, and discovering new horizons. Follow-up research on employees who have been forced to change jobs has consistently found that the majority of them move on to far better careers than they had before. Many look back on the period of distress as an excellent learning process. Overcoming adversity creates a new appreciation of one's emotional reserves and strength to withstand stress. Change forces one to appreciate the more basic joys of life, such as creativity, health, and the ability to recognize new opportunities.

In one case, a Dragon boss targeted a marketing analyst because of his knowledge base. The idea that marketing/sales and production must work together was a threat to the Dragon, and the analyst was targeted for destruction even though it would have looked very bad if he had been terminated. The interesting point about the case was that after being pushed out, with a resignation on his own (to keep the Dragon from looking bad), the analyst accepted a position with a competitor. His genuine ideas about working relationships and partnerships (not just teamwork) brought about several promotions. His new company captured a large percentage of the market, thus taking away a substantial amount of business from his former employer. His career was very positive with the new company in ways that he had never dreamed possible.

Find Your Options

Look for ways to deal with your distressing situation and appreciate your ability to make choices. The freedom to choose is the key to turning distress into positive, focused energy. Just knowing that there are answers to your pain often brings relief to the confusion and gives direction to your personal decision-making powers.

Decisions Are Destiny in Progress

There are an unlimited number of options from which to make decisions. Some decisions are mundane, and some are vital to the future. No person can predict what label today's decision will wear tomorrow. Yesterday is already history, and tomorrow is always a mystery; it is today that demands our best. To make better decisions when under extremely stressful conditions, here is some good advice from several old proverbs:

- Remember that deciding not to decide is a decision.
- Make a decision if you must but reserve the option to re-decide.
- Deliberation is not delaying.
- Where duty is plain, delay is dangerous; where it is not, delay may be wise and safe.

Pace Your Stress

If you are finding it difficult to pay attention to each particular step in large assignments, try a new approach. Rather than add tension to your life by concentrating your energy on outcome goals, focus on the milestones but deal with the daily choices.

- Clarify goals. Make sure that you have a clear idea of the project's goals and that you know the purpose behind your assigned task.
- Anticipate the hurdles. If the workplace is dysfunctional, there will be many obstacles to overcome.
- See those obstacles as challenges and be prepared to focus your energy productively.
- Stay current. Organize your workflow by prioritizing tasks according to deadlines.
- Do not be sidetracked by Dragon smoke. Concentrate on the daily choices you have and make each decision in terms of what you think is best.

While You Are Reading, Learning, and Exploring, Pay Attention to:

Variety

If you have a desk job, adding positive stress to your life in the form of physical exercise will help you. If you enjoy athletics, try running, hiking, or biking. However, if you detest athletics, your emotions will sabotage your efforts. You may add variety to your routine by dancing or playing a musical instrument. Perhaps volunteering as a playground supervisor at the local park or becoming the kids' hockey coach would be your style. Maintaining your interests and having a balance between work and play is important during stressful times. Whatever you choose, be sure that it is something you like to do. Developing your hobbies and interests will reduce stress and help you keep things in perspective.

Sleep

The more scientists learn about neurological functioning, the more they recognize the value of sleep to restore the intellect, refresh the emotions, and provide strength to deal more effectively with stresses. To keep up with today's workday pace, most adults need nearly nine to ten hours of rest. This need is even greater when extreme stress and third-degree anger are part of the picture.

What if you are too stressed to sleep? Try talking yourself into relaxing. The fascinating part of the rather clumsy mind-body-emotion process is that the mind can trick the autonomic system into replacing alarm reactions with more positive feelings that support relaxation, letting go, and energy renewal.

Self-Talk

The quickest way to relax and renew is by self-direction. Learning how to shut down, turn off, and re-energize is a simple skill that anyone can learn with just a little guidance and practice. Try this self-guided relaxation exercise for a starter. You may want to follow the directions using your softest, slowest, most relaxing voice or, if you prefer, just use unspoken self-talk. You might even want to prepare an audio tape of the directions.

1. Position yourself in a quiet place, preferably lying on the floor with arms comfortably outstretched and legs slightly apart but relaxed. You may want a soft pillow or a folded towel to support your neck. Pay attention to your breathing until you are able to exhale long, refreshing breaths.

2. Slowly take a mental journey through your body. Start by giving your toes, feet, and legs permission to relax and then proceed toward your neck and head. Imagine discarding your negative thoughts and feelings into an imaginary wastebasket one by one until your mind is able to relax. Now, see yourself setting the wastebasket outside and feel your tension disappear as you close your door against the outside world. Pay attention to your calm, safe, peaceful feelings of contentment and enjoy being aware of your personal pleasure as you begin to feel relaxed.

3. Now, slowly become aware of your face and neck. Make a frown, smile, scrunch up your neck and facial muscles tightly. Hold it for a few seconds and then relax. Feel the tension roll away. Like drops of moisture in a warm refreshing shower, allow the tension to drain away and disappear.

4. Next, focus on your shoulders, arms, and hands. Tighten your muscles, inhale, hold it, and then relax as you exhale. Take a mental journey through both arms, making sure that each muscle gets the message to relax completely as you feel tension dissolve.

5. Proceed down through the body, focusing on the chest, abdominal, and groin areas. Then focus on the legs, feet, and toes by tensing the muscles and then relaxing them. Feel the tension drain away.

6. Take a quick journey through your body, making sure that every muscle is completely relaxed. When a thought comes into your

mind, just allow it to pass through and leave without disturbing your rest.

7. Now open your eyes widely and turn your concentration to a particular spot on the ceiling above you. Keep staring at the ceiling. Feel the tension in your eyelids until they become heavy. Then allow them to close naturally and peacefully. Relax deeply. Continue to enjoy your peaceful moments for as long as you wish. If sleep comes, welcome it. You will awaken refreshed with renewed energy and a more positive attitude when your body is ready.

You will find that with practice you will only need to think about the above process and then begin to relax very quickly starting at steps six and seven. For most people, fifteen minutes of self-directed relaxation equals about three hours of sleep.

Exercise

Walking the equivalent of at least two miles a day is a minimum for good health. Aerobics, bicycling, jogging, or any other form of exercise you enjoy helps strengthen your cardiovascular system and makes you more resilient against negative effects of stress. Participating in activities such as yoga, kickboxing, sports, etc. may help you release built-up stress and vent emotions in a safe manner. Physical activity can help you keep a more positive attitude and reduce the amount of stress you feel.

Diet

This is not the time to go on a crash diet. However, it is the time to make sure that you are eating foods rich in vitamins, minerals, and low in saturated fats. To combat stress, you need excellent nutrition. Do not settle for less than a balanced amount of proteins, carbohydrates, vegetables, fruits, and grains. This is not the time for food binges and not a time for chocolate, sugars, and food additives.

Those neurons need all the help they can get. Skip the big meals, the buffets, and grandma's cooking. Eat lightly and often. Treat yourself to a snack about every two hours to raise your metabolic rate and stabilize your energy. Low-sugar, nutritious snacks improve your mood and reduce the tendency toward food cravings when under pressure.

Clutch Activities

You should practice shifting gears between work and home. *Gear down* by leaving your Dragon at work. Prepare to enjoy your family and friends at home. To *gear down,* try some of the following:

- Listen to your favorite music on the way home.
- Give yourself 20 minutes of in-the-den or in-the-bedroom rest and isolation upon arrival and then enjoy the family.
- Stop by the health club for a great workout followed by a swim or sauna.
- Pick up inexpensive surprises for your loved ones.
- Skip the crowded freeways and take the scenic route home. Enjoy the ride.

Gear up by preparing for the stress that you are sure to experience in the workplace.

- Start your day with a vigorous swim.
- Listen to your favorite CD's on the way to work.
- Allow more than adequate time to arrive. Take the scenic route or have breakfast with your friends.
- Arrive early enough to give yourself some quiet time before organizing your day.
- Smile and greet your coworkers cordially. Remember, you are sharing the same workplace and probably the same stresses.

For more suggestions, see Step V, Take Action.

Step III Summary

Unlike animals, humans have an incredible system of feelings and thoughts that come into play when we sense danger. One such alarm system is the GAS, our automatic fight-or-flight feelings that are often identified as anger, misdirected fear, or stress. Under subtle or continued threat, this defensive system is felt as distress. We seem to vacillate back and forth between emotions due to the confusion of thoughts and feelings that are simultaneously flooding our awareness. Victims of abuse report similar emotional patterns, whether the abuse is in the family, on the job, or in prisoner-of-war camps. The overall intellectual state is confusion, but the basic emotions range from anger and fear to depression.

Let Your Feelings Be Your Guide

- First-degree anger alerts you to threats.
- Second-degree anger informs you of a serious problem that needs immediate attention.
- Third-degree anger, with suicidal ideation and calls for action, has the potential for violence or depression.

Discussion

Exercise I

How intense are your feelings of anger on the job?

First-degree anger:

Ticked off and annoyed occasionally. I am checking to be sure that I am not being groomed for victimization.

Second-degree anger:

Recurring anger interferes with my performance. I must identify the problem that my anger is warning me about and see what can be done to resolve the issue(s).

Third-degree anger:

Intolerable stress interferes with my life. I am experiencing underlying feelings of fear, loss, and betrayal. I must take definite steps toward making changes. Time is running out.

What is your anger telling you about your workplace? How can you use your anger alarm to reduce confusion and give direction to career planning?

Exercise 2

a. What are some forms of positive stress in your life?

b. How can positive stress help one to tolerate the negative stresses most of us endure in our daily lives?

c. What is one negative stress that you wish to resolve? Can you identify the source of the stress?

d. What is one positive stress that you could add to your life if you wished to do so?

Exercise 3

a. What feelings can you identify that accompany your workplace experience?

b. Are your workplace stresses positive or negative?

c. What are your most intense feelings in the workplace?

Step IV

Disarm the Dragons

In Step IV, we will expose the truth about what Dragons actually do to victimize people and give information on how to disarm Dragons. There are four parts to this step:

Chapter 8, **Hang on to Your Beliefs,** describes the classic brainwashing techniques that Dragons use to manipulate victims. They attack basic belief systems and thus gain control over a victim's will to resist. Once intended victims recognize Dragon smoke for what it really is (the irrational thoughts that the Dragon wants them to believe), they can learn to counteract abuse by replacing the smoke with rational thoughts. With the background information about tracking Dragons in the workplace, as well as new knowledge on how to keep one's basic belief system in place, targeted victims will be able to tame the Dragon and prevent future attacks.

In Chapter 9, **Dragon Fire Extinguishers**, we describe the types of pressure that Dragons use on victims. With such ploys identified, abusive strategies tend to lose effectiveness, thus their Dragon fire (techniques) and its smoke (mystification) are extinguished. We have included several examples in this chapter that demonstrate effective methods of resisting the most common types of pressures and weapons, which include coercion, gang-ups, double binds, "why" daggers, and "you" guns.

Chapter 10 focuses on the **Subtle Abuse** of power. When does "just doing business" become abuse? The most frequent forms of abusive power that Dragons use include: discrimination, isolation, economic abuse, and heavy workloads. Here again, we will give you examples and ideas for handling each of these problems in the workplace.

Chapter 11 addresses **Deliberate Abuse**. When suggestions turn to harassment, the victim has usually been designated as Dragon food and is being forced out. In this chapter, we present sexual harassment, transfers that are not requested, and general psychological tormenting, as well as methods for counteracting such abuses.

Chapter 8

Hang on to Your Beliefs

Now that we have looked carefully at your emotions, the next step in sorting out the confusion is to pin down reality. Reality is what *Dragons actually do* and what it is that *victims typically think.* The interaction between the two constitutes a subtle pattern of abuse characteristics in the workplace.

Dragons do torment their victims psychologically with verbal attacks (Dragon fire), but they also use classic brainwashing to change their victim's basic belief systems. The process begins slowly with subtle remarks that are strategically spaced apart to ensure that the victim does not comprehend what is happening. The victim does know that something is wrong but cannot identify it! With an intentional increase in frequency, the brainwashing involves a mental torture routine designed to:

- Induce fear or threaten and punish until victims assume the blame for their own abuse and are silenced by shame or guilt.
- Undermine their will to resist and then forbid them to do so.
- Attack the victims' basic belief systems until seeds of fear become subliminal influences that enslave victims.

(See Chapter 3, Signature Pattern No. 6, Numbing.)

Dragons, like abusers everywhere, trap victims by manipulating them into believing the abusive propaganda (Dragon smoke), thus compromising the victims' values and attacking self-esteem. Once victims believe the problem is their own fault, they stop trying to rectify the situation.

> Jennifer was a staff assistant for a marketing manager at a shipping company. She had refused advances and requests for an affair. Thus, she had been set up as Dragon food. The manager at first began to accuse her of trying to avoid him but such was not the case.

> Jennifer was rather bewildered about the accusations. The next step involved accusations of not completing work in a timely manner. The negative comments and various types of accusations increased in frequency over time, with Jennifer believing it was her own fault. Fortunately, she was able to secure a different position with another company. A few years later, she woke up one morning with the realization of what had happened to her. Jennifer indicated that no one would believe how smooth the boss was in creating an atmosphere in which she believed she was absolutely worthless.

You can counter such negative brainwashing by your own brand of positive affirmations. Your beliefs can be far more powerful than the words of another person, especially when you have the personal freedom to choose whether or not to leave the situation. For example, the boss is attacking you with a series of derogatory comments and insults (Dragon fire). The frequency of such remarks has increased, and you now realize what is happening. You can counter with your reasoning process. This requires identifying the problem, recognizing what you are feeling and thinking, and focusing energy in a positive manner.

Dragon Smoke

These are the irrational thoughts that the Dragon wants you to have. When you believe the negative implications about yourself, you are easier to manipulate. Such thoughts sound like this:

It is entirely my fault. I should never make anyone furious. I deserve to be punished. I am a failure. I cannot understand why the boss is so angry, so I must be stupid. I deserve all the rotten names in the book. The boss is so smart, so powerful, and so important that my entire career is in her hands. I hope I don't get fired. It would mean that I am a failure.

Dragon-Taming Thoughts

These are rational replacement thoughts to substitute for the negative Dragon smoke. They combat the Dragon's propaganda because they discredit it. Dragon-taming thoughts sound something like this:

Words do not hurt unless I believe them. The boss might have an anger problem or this could be an act aimed at my emotions. The boss is having a tantrum and inviting me into an anger dance, but I have a right to decline the invitation. Sorry Boss, I choose to use my energy for pleasure not pain. I will just wait until your *storming* is over, and if I think it is worth my time, I will follow up with you when you are calm.

Dragon-Proofing Beliefs

These thoughts acknowledge your feelings in a rational way and allow you to maintain your self-confidence, something that dispels Dragon smoke. These beliefs can help to armor you against future attacks. They may include a dialogue such as this:

I'm a good person, but I can make mistakes. I have a right to feel anger but not on your time schedule. I feel first-degree anger, and it is annoying but certainly not life threatening. I can handle it. If this happens again, I will need to level with you. I will wait to see what happens when you are calm and we have an opportunity to explore the problem.

Comments

You can realize that the boss's blood pressure is probably racing out of control. You can feel good about your own emotional control as you simply refuse to let the situation affect your composure. Calmly focus on locating the problem that may have contributed to the outburst.

The difficulty usually lies in the abuser's unique pattern of thinking and bizarre belief system. If your boss is a true Dragon and you try to explore the problem that is triggering your anger, you are sure to be confused because if you are not a Dragon, you will not think like one. It will be hard for you to imagine a Dragon's thinking process.

Any attempt to discuss the incident later when your boss is calm, constitutes a threat. The most likely result will be another attack on your feelings, self-esteem, and beliefs. You will find that the Dragon will abuse power by degrading you, intimidating with daggers like "why" questions, shooting at your self-esteem with the "you" gun, finding fault, and blaming. These abusers may use obscene language, name-calling, and ridicule as additional power plays.

If you feel angry, congratulations! Your warning system is in good working order. You are not yet silenced by fear or coerced by intimidation. The typical Dragon uses and abuses power in the workplace in the hopes that you will be frightened into irrational thinking. Rational thinking is the antidote to power plays. So hang on to your rational thinking as you explore the crazy thoughts that the Dragon wants you to accept as true.

Stay in touch with your true beliefs. Use your own personal power to choose, to decide, and to act. Do it on your own time and in your own way, without the pressure from any Dragon.

An Example in the Criminal Justice System

Potential abusers often seek out paramilitary or other environments with rigid power hierarchies, such as law enforcement, corporate bureaucracies, and corrections. Some who are successful in police work, for example, share with Dragons a love of danger, a desire to intimidate with terror, and a lust for power. They enjoy their own stress-related hormone surges and gradually dull their softer feelings, while increasing their controlled-anger responses. It is not uncommon to hear about the "hardness" of career police, military, and corrections officers.

Careers in criminal justice and law enforcement are seedbeds for job stress. Constantly surrounded by criminal behavior, the individual must have an excellent grasp of the law, as well as a solid belief system. This career calls for the finest in moral values, clearly defined ethical standards, and unusual courage in order to handle the endless power-related choices that at times involve split-second decisions. Simply doing the daily job requires personal power plays ranging from verbal commands to physical force. Under such circumstances it is quite easy to suffer genuine moral conflicts and confusion about one's belief system, even when there are no Dragons with which to contend.

Where there is a Dragon in residence, however, the entire system can turn deadly. The good guys get broad brushed along with the Doorkeepers. The simple stress becomes intolerable distress, morale plummets, and the entire workplace feels the impact.

Dragon Proofing Yourself: The Antidote to Dragon Smoke

A well-structured belief system allows a person to distinguish between right and wrong, allowing moral and ethical behavior to be possible. Abusers are experts at mystification and attacking the belief system. We will now look at the compounded stresses of an employee in law enforcement when a Dragon is involved.

Don's Story:

Don, a rookie police officer, went through the customary training sessions. They prepared him to carry a weapon and to understand legal and discrimination issues. His training included self-defense, subduing and handcuffing, interrogation, reporting procedures, and related duties. As an adjunct to human rights training, he learned among other things how to *help* the suspect into the squad car by inserting his thumbs deeply into the subject's ears and/or eyes, causing severe pain with no visible bruises. He learned several versions of "slamming:" (1) suddenly slamming on the brakes, thereby letting the momentum thrust the prisoner headlong into the steel grating, (2) slamming body parts in doors *by accident* and then apologizing, and (3) slamming the head against anything that would cause pain. He learned how to prod an unwilling, handcuffed suspect with the arms pulled behind and then forced overhead. Dragging them in this manner causes the weight of the body to disjoint the shoulders and causes extreme pain but leaves no visible signs of abuse.

Don learned about the *blue wall of silence*, his guarantee that his partner's supportive duty logs, reports, testimony, or silence would nullify any bruises, cuts, or other evidence of police brutality. At first, he was thrilled at being an insider, privy to the unwritten code of conduct. At first, he considered the bizarre examples to be just exaggerated gossip. He was shocked but kept silent.

He thoroughly enjoyed the power of his uniform to attract attention, especially when it involved the favorable attention of young, vulnerable ladies. After a few years on the job, he quietly left his position. This man, who several years earlier had achieved public recognition for his fine citizenship, surrendered his potentially fulfilling career in law enforcement. He left rather than compromise his values by condoning, either with silence or capitulation, the brutality he saw occurring. Rather than risk retaliation by becoming a whistle-blower or a victim himself, he resigned. Without his knowledge, he had been tested for Doorkeeper status. (See Chapter 3, Signature Pattern No. 3, Assessment.)

The Test:

1. Will You Place Yourself In A Vulnerable Position?

Don passed with flying colors. He was given inside information and groomed. The lures were the thrill of power, money, and a beckoning career. He was tempted to set aside his personal beliefs long enough to become vulnerable to a new belief system, one not diametrically opposed to criminal behavior but on the right side of the law. He enjoyed the role of being a Robin Hood, a legitimate bully.

2. Will You Condone Abuse by Witnessing Others Being Abused or Join in the Abusing with Me?

Don passed marginally. At first, this former halfback enjoyed the physical self-defense training. He reconsidered when he witnessed unwarranted brutality by other officers, realized that his job included more than just talk, and understood that he would be required to compromise his beliefs. For a short period, he willingly participated in activities that he previously considered immoral, but he generally balked at actually doing or witnessing behavior that he felt was illegal or unethical.

3. Will You Keep Silent?

He passed. He never discussed his conflicts, pressures, or insights while on the job or after he left.

4. Will You Protect The Dragon And The System?

He failed. He was unwilling to protect the Dragon and decided that he could not be a part of the system, so he left. To confront the system would have taken more courage than he had and more evidence than he could provide. After all, he had joined in long enough to be *hooked,* and his guilt silenced him, but he was alert enough not to permit himself to be Dragon food. Eventually, and without his help, the system changed. The Dragon left, but nobody ever broke the blue wall of silence within this particular police force. Don did, however, enter into personal, couples, and family therapy in order to deal with the aftermath at home. Gradually, he had become physically abusive and unfaithful, but he blamed it all on *job stress.*

Dragon Smoke

Here are the irrational thoughts that the Dragon wanted Don to think:

Everyone is corrupt; the whole system is on the take. This is the *real* world; so forget about what you learned in Sunday school. Here we have our own laws and our own ways of doing what needs to be done. Sometimes we do whatever it takes, but, as long as we do it to a bad guy, might makes right.

I must listen to my superior. It is right that he has complete power over me and everyone else in order to do justice. I am only a small cog in the machine, and if I break, I will be replaced. Sometimes there will be mistakes, but I am loyal. My boss's screams of "You just don't get it, do you!" translate into "You have been warned that there are *no mistakes here.* Cover up. Keep the silence, and you're safe. Break the silence, and you're through."

If I do not do as I am told, or if I tell anyone, I'm a rat. I deserve to be ostracized, punished, blackballed, fired, or even killed. I must always cover up for the Dragon, and he will cover for me. I must maintain the blue wall of silence, yet deny that such a wall exists or has ever existed.

Dragon-Taming Thoughts

What thoughts could Don use to counteract the irrational thoughts? Here are our answers:

I am responsible for upholding the law. It is difficult to know the difference between right and wrong, especially when I must control or overcome suspects while keeping my partners and myself as safe as possible. I may make some mistakes, but I try to keep my suspects' safety and rights in mind, as well as my own.

My job is risky, and trust is absolutely necessary in this line of work. Secrets cannot exist in a trusting relationship, and my life depends on that trust. If I am pressured or threatened to compromise my beliefs and values by keeping silent, then I am risking my life. I am being victimized.

Dragon-Proofing Beliefs

These beliefs form the basis for determining right from wrong.

People are innocent until proven guilty. We are a society of laws. Law enforcement must never be above the law. I will not be a part of anything illegal, immoral, or unethical. When the lines are blurred, I will search out any needed information, make a judgment call, and be responsible for everything I do and say. I am not willing to bet my life on a backup officer whom I cannot trust.

Comments

There are certain acts that are clearly criminal and abusive. In the free world, people in law enforcement have the law on their side, as long as they are not Doorkeepers. This means that they have not submitted to intimidation and have chosen not to cover up or remain silent about abuse of power within their workplaces. A Dragon without Doorkeepers is helpless. Being unwilling to (1) witness, (2) be a part of, or (3) remain silent about Dragon acts is the only way to ensure healthy trust among all employees within an organization.

Understanding the signature patterns of Dragons and discovering their tracks are the early steps toward keeping the workplace safe. Designing some protections for corrections and law enforcement personnel against abuse of power and identifying more appropriate choices in resisting corruption are crucial ingredients in the organization of any police force. Such steps can leave any Dragon without Doorkeepers.

The problem is, however, that when the Dragon represents the law, it is unprofitable for citizens to call the police for help. Fortunately, the press, public exposure, and media coverage following a particularly outrageous incident of police brutality can set the wheels of justice into action and put an end to Dragons' and Doorkeepers' opportunities. As in any corporation that allows a dysfunctional work environment, the best people - those dedicated to the highest principles of morality and justice - leave, transfer, or succumb to "job stress." Many try to fit shattered pieces of their lives back together in therapy, never realizing that they have been Dragon food.

Summary

Dragons torment their victims psychologically with classic brainwashing techniques. They manipulate victims into believing negative propaganda (Dragon smoke) in order to gain and maintain control.

Discussion

- Were you subjected to the *test* and how did you fare? (Refer to Chapter 3, Signature Pattern No. 3, Assessment.)

Because the process is so smooth and subtle, a candidate for grooming rarely recognizes the test. Typically, it is discovered in retrospect. Think back to the time when you were new on the job. Were you subjected to any informal situation or given any "confidential" information - a "dirty secret" - that made you feel uncomfortable? If so, you could have been taking the test. How did you do?

1. Did you keep the secret?
2. Did you compromise your ethics or values?
3. Did you join in and place yourself in a vulnerable position?
4. Do you feel that you were being groomed?

If you answered "yes" to question one, you have essentially passed the test from the Dragon's viewpoint. If you answered "no" to questions two and three, it could be a clear signal that you may have been selected for Dragon food and are vulnerable to abuse. If you answered "yes" to the fourth question, it means that the Dragon considers you to have passed the test, and you will be counted on to abuse other people.

Exercise:

My Irrational Thoughts were:

What was the Dragon Smoke?

What did the Dragon or Doorkeeper want you to believe?

My Rational, Dragon-Taming Replacement Thoughts are now:

My Dragon-Proofing Beliefs, Values, Ethics, Judgments are:

My Test Situation was:

Chapter 9

Dragon Fire Extinguishers

When one is able to identify a Dragon's ploys and mind-twisting techniques (Dragon fire), one can begin to extinguish the fire and start planning ways to recover. This chapter outlines Dragon-taming thoughts and Dragon-proofing beliefs, which create a "Dragon fire extinguisher" with which to combat abuse.

Are You Pressured Either Verbally or Nonverbally to Do Things Against Your Will?

Toxic Pressures

Instead of being open and honest with all requests and demands, an abusive boss will often resort to verbal or nonverbal coercive pressures. Often, all a Dragon has to do is imply that something should be done and that the Dragon has enough power to expect results. In most cases, these demands are at odds with the employee's sense of morality. Sometimes, an employee is expected to abuse other people in the company, go to taverns instead of meetings out of town, attend or take part in sexual parties, or commit dishonest acts on behalf of the Dragon.

Mary Lou, an executive secretary, had the responsibility of signing purchase orders for general office supplies. Her Dragon boss was involved in a company swindle wherein he created a bogus supply company. He wanted Mary Lou to sign the purchase orders, which set in motion the process for company checks to be mailed to the bogus company with an out-of-town address. The checks were actually picked up by the boss and deposited into his secret bank account.

When Mary Lou discovered the ploy, she refused to sign any more purchase orders for the false company.

Dragon Boss: You'll sign these PO's if you know what's good for you.

Mary Lou: You know as well as I do that no such company exists, and I will not be part of such a scheme. If the company finds out, I will be in serious trouble.

Dragon Boss: That's not your problem. Just scribble your name so nobody can recognize it and trace it to you. If they do, I will take care of it.

Mary Lou refused to sign her name, and from that point on, the boss made her life miserable. He constantly disapproved of everything, from her hair to her attitude. She soon resigned for what she regarded as safety reasons. She was one of those slated for Dragon food who fortunately moved on to a better job. However, the mystified company she left behind lost an honest and valuable employee.

Dragon Smoke

Irrational thoughts that the Dragon wanted Mary Lou to think:

I'm just taking orders, so what do I care whether or not my job is strictly legal? The boss certainly is clever. Purchasing from a bogus company and then having the money transferred to his secret account is a good way to hide extra money for both of us. It is not my place to judge anyone. As long as I am getting paid well, I am thrilled that he has taken me into his confidence. I will do as I am told without questioning. After all, my boss said he would take care of me if there were any problems. As his executive secretary, I am the only one in whom he can confide. Yes, I will prove to him that I am a *team player,* and he will stop pressuring me so much. Even legitimate raises will come easily from now on, now that I'm an insider.

Dragon-Taming Thoughts

Rational replacement thoughts:

Bogus purchase orders are illegal. I am not willing to be part of an illegal scheme. However, I had better check with my boss for more details or get his specific orders in writing before I jump to the conclusion that this deal is not legitimate. In the meantime, I will not sign my name to questionable purchase orders. I will have a tough time saying "no" without risking my job, so I had better stall for a time while I document everything in my diary.

I will try saying, "As your executive secretary, I appreciate your trust, but being a cautious sort of person, I need some more information about this proposal. I am confused. You dictate, and I will write down exactly what it is that you expect me to do, and I will get back to you with any questions that I have. In the meantime, will you please sign off on all the PO's until we decide exactly how we will handle them in the future?"

Dragon-Proofing Beliefs

I am an honest person. I have the right to refuse to participate in any questionable scheme that I believe is dishonest. My boss has no right to pressure me into signing my name to anything illegitimate. I believe in getting all of the details before jumping to conclusions about another person's intentions.

Comments

A legitimate boss who is about to make a serious mistake will appreciate your efforts to slow down the process with your request to document details. This boss will be quite willing to give you information and time to discuss your questions and will also allow you to say "no" graciously.

A Dragon will attempt to intimidate you, pressure you, or simply refuse to acknowledge your request. If you allow yourself to be coerced into activities that are dishonest, illegal, or against your moral code, the Dragon will be the first to blame you for the very actions that you were demanded to take. The Dragon, with the support of the Doorkeepers, will cover tracks and target you for victimization and constructive dismissal. You will be Dragon food.

Have You Experienced the "Gang-Up" Technique?

(See Chapter 3, Signature Pattern No. 6, Numbing and Nullifying.)

We have all heard bosses say, "If you have a problem on the job, tell me. Then we'll see if it can be straightened out. My door is always open." Both sincere and insincere bosses commonly express this invitation. When a Dragon issues this statement, it is always a lie.

What happens when an employee who is targeted for abuse requests a meeting with a Dragon to clarify a situation? To begin with, Doorkeepers are included in the meeting, and they set the tone. The meeting is usually a series of systematic power plays, with the Dragon and Doorkeepers tossing the victim back and forth with a confusing barrage of intimidating remarks that have no substance. Doorkeepers not only intimidate, but they also lie for the Dragon. Afterward, they will help the Dragon by inventing false descriptions of what the victim said or did at this particular meeting. A seemingly confidential meeting with the Dragon turns out to be a gang-up session with an outnumbered victim. For example:

> Franklin, a marketing-research specialist, was concerned about the customer service provided for a tool-and-die company. At the time, Franklin did not realize that he had already been set up for victimization.
>
> Franklin was unsuccessful in his attempts to contact the Assistant Vice President, Ginger. Phone calls and e-mail went unanswered. Therefore, Franklin made an

appointment for a personal meeting with Ginger through the AVP's secretary. Upon arriving at the meeting, he was told that it had been canceled and was referred to Ginger's assistant. When Franklin explained the situation to the assistant, she was completely confused, had received no message about the problem or the meeting, and could not offer any help.

The next day Franklin noticed that Ginger's office door was open, so he entered.

Franklin: Sorry you couldn't meet with me yesterday, but I need to talk to you about A&B Tool and Die.

Ginger: Why not come in now? You know my door is always open!

Franklin: But you have other people here, and I don't want to interrupt.

Ginger: No problem. We can discuss anything.

Franklin: With the downsizing that we just went through, it turns out that Marketing has oversold our current capacity to produce. We are going to lose A&B Tool and Die, and they have a twenty-year history with us. What would you suggest for our next step?

Ginger sat back in silence and squinted her eyes at Franklin.

Ginger: Why did you let this problem exist for such a long time?

(Note the phrase "long time," which was not true. The downsizing had taken place only a short time ago, but it was impacting the company's ability to fill customer orders on a timely basis. The statement was designed to confuse the victim.)

Franklin: I had nothing to do with the problem. I am the Research Analyst, and I have tried to contact you several times about it.

Ginger: You didn't answer my question. We are not talking about my returning your calls; we are talking about your failure.

(Notice the boss's inadvertent admission about not returning the calls and her blaming the messenger who is, in this case, the Dragon's newest victim.)

Franklin: What failure?

Doorkeeper 1: Your failure to identify the problem and bring it to the Assistant Vice President in a timely manner.

Franklin: But I tried . . . (Doorkeeper 2 cuts in.)

Doorkeeper 2: Quite to the contrary. If you did indeed call, why didn't you keep calling?

(Periodically during this "tossing back and forth" technique, the two Doorkeepers would smile at each other, sending still another nonverbal "we're going to get you" message to Franklin.)

Franklin: You are missing the point. I tried very hard to . . .

Ginger: Why did you let this problem exist in the first place?

(The parrot-like questions are designed to support the Dragon while attacking the victim.)

Franklin: That is why I tried to contact you as long as two months ago . . .

Ginger: I received no such messages.

Franklin: I talked to your voice mail and secretary...

Ginger: (speaking in a very vicious tone) Don't you dare put my secretary between us!

Totally bewildered at this point, Franklin could no longer respond logically. The questions kept coming, and each question was further from the specific topic. Soon the three bullies even began bringing up examples of Franklin's supposed failures in other areas. The meeting became a lopsided victory as the Dragon and Doorkeepers played their game of *attacking* the victim and *avoiding* the problem.

You might want to compare your *reality* with the Dragon's *reality*. So the logical thing is to ask questions - anyone knows that! You attempt to set up a private meeting. Instead of clearing up the confusion, you are in for an unpleasant surprise. You might not even be allowed to meet with the supervisor. Instead, a Doorkeeper might intervene. If you do manage to engage your Dragon in a meeting, the results can be just as unsatisfactory. With the help of Doorkeepers, the Dragon will engage you in a lopsided conversation to make you feel insecure, dependent, and subservient. There might be veiled threats that your job is on the line. Words can be manipulated, and the subject might be changed at a bewildering pace until you are confused about what is actually being discussed. As topics rapidly change, you might be asked questions without being given time to think through your answers. This ploy is designed to make you look and feel stupid. These manipulators are proficient at attacking victims and triggering feelings of anger and fear in order to undercut their victims' logic.

This gang-up technique is especially brutal in public places such as lunchrooms or hallways where an audience is available to witness the embarrassment of the victim. The public gang-up sends clear messages that this employee is now an outsider and that anyone not wishing to be next would be wise to shun the employee.

Dragon Smoke

Irrational ideas that the Dragon wants you to think:

I just overstepped a boundary. I should not have tried to talk to the boss. I am stupid for asking questions. From now on, I will keep my mouth shut and just take orders. If I am so stupid that I didn't know there was a boundary, I deserve to be punished. It was my fault. The whole gang agreed with each other, so I must be completely out of order. I thought the boss said to come to him for answers, but I guess I was wrong. I hope the boss is not going to fire me. I have been ridiculed. How devastating! I could be in for much worse treatment from all of them if I ask any more questions.

Dragon-Taming Thoughts

Rational replacement thoughts:

Asking for clarification about problem areas or my job status is logical but apparently is threatening to the boss. So what did I learn for next time? Experiencing a gang-up warns me that my boss has Doorkeepers for some reason. I doubt that I could be important enough to warrant the attention of three people, so I will be alert for additional attempts at victimization. From the tone of the gang-up, I can hypothesize that I have been selected for Dragon food and that they want me to keep quiet or resign. Apparently I have raised an issue connected to something illegal or unethical or some type of huge management error that can never be admitted. So I will temporarily keep my mouth closed and my eyes and ears open, but the experience goes into my Dragon diary *right now*!

Dragon-Proofing Beliefs

Courage is willingness to take risks. I do have courage. I can differentiate between risks that are worth it and those that are not. I have decided that risking ridicule by asking directly about a crucial problem is assertive and well worth the risk, because this behavior will let the boss know where I stand and avoids compromising my honesty and values.

Comments

Bullies are cowards who abuse power and victimize others; gang-ups are their classic tools. Once you recognize this strategy, your anger alarm goes off, and you can clearly recognize the first stage of victimization. Let them rage and then learn what you can from their behavior. Recognize the gang-up but do not let the ridicule throw you. They are just playing power games intended to intimidate you.

Hunt for further evidence that you are being groomed or tested as a potential Doorkeeper or that you are targeted as Dragon food. Use strong, principled assertion to remove yourself from either position. Keep your eyes open for the secret information or activities that their system is set up to protect. This includes a lack of knowledge about the company and/or customers and clients.

Does the Boss Degrade You?

(See Chapter 3, Signature Pattern No. 6, Numbing and Nullifying.)
(See Chapter 4, Game No. 3, Heads I Win, Tails You Lose.)

Belittling and degrading employees in order to make them feel foolish is an abuse of power. Dragons frequently resort to this tactic in attempts to attack a victim's self-concept. Belittling makes the targeted employee less likely to have the courage to express ideas. Therefore, it decreases opportunities for creativity and open discussion. At the core of such degradation is public humiliation for the victim. For the abuser, there is the feeling of domination over others.

In a typical belittling session, the Dragon will create both a double-bind situation that says, "Damned if you do, damned if you don't" and also a three-step punishment process that goes like this:

- *Step 1* Belittle and ridicule the victim for new ideas that are presented to the Dragon. The victim learns that new ideas bring punishment, and therefore, it is best to remain quiet.
- *Step 2* Belittle and ridicule the victim for not presenting new ideas. Then, the confused victim begins distancing away from the abusers.
- *Step 3* Belittle and degrade the victim for not being enthusiastic, proactive, and able to "move into the future" with the rest of the Doorkeeper group.

Do you feel as though your supervisors do not take you seriously? You might know that the clients or customers respect you and that you have a great deal to contribute. Your customer relations are positive, and through these relations, you have gained insight into better ways to serve clients while benefiting the company's profit ratio. Can you answer "yes" to any of the following questions?

- Are your suggestions ignored or belittled while the Doorkeepers' ideas are praised and adopted even though they are inferior to or simply a reiteration of your own ideas? (For example, your idea is ridiculed, but a Doorkeeper makes the same suggestion two weeks later and is praised publicly for it.)
- Are you the scapegoat when the Dragon's suggestions fail to produce?
- Are you blamed for making poor suggestions in the first place?

If any of these ploys are occurring, do not be too quick to take personal responsibility for the abusers' actions. Do not accept their claims about your inability to create good ideas for the company. You must believe in yourself. If your boss is a Dragon, chances are that you are being set up for failure and constructive dismissal.

When Dragons get tired of the double-bind degradation game, they obsessively keep track of your mistakes. All humans make them, and people under pressure often make even more. The abusive boss can always use this fresh stockpile of evidence to attack you.

Dragon Smoke

Irrational thoughts that the boss wants you to think:

I must do everything perfectly or suffer the consequences of well-deserved public degradation. Since I made one mistake, I will certainly make more mistakes. I am helpless and stupid. I must follow the boss's orders exactly, without thinking or feeling. I must degrade myself, just as the boss degrades me. My entire future depends on pleasing my boss and not provoking anger. I must work harder, longer, do exactly as I am told, and never make another mistake.

Dragon-Taming Thoughts

Rational replacement thoughts:

I want to do things well. I am a valuable person developing skill in working under difficult circumstances. The responsibility for the boss's anger belongs to the boss. Mistakes aren't bad; they are human errors that contribute to growth.

Just because the Dragon rages, that does not mean that I have to repeat the verbal abuse to myself. I am human, and all humans are imperfect. I will fix the mistakes if possible. I have the strength to honor the truth while believing in myself. I can handle adversity, and I can handle having made an honest mistake.

Dragon-Proofing Beliefs

A mistake is by definition an accident. All humans make them from time to time. Part of my enjoyment of life is strengthening personal skills and decreasing mistakes. I am a person of worth, and I value my intelligence. I also value what I learn from my mistakes. I take full responsibility for any negative consequences that result from my mistakes and do my best to rectify any damages. I constantly work toward eliminating as many mistakes as possible from my performance. I also know that some creative breakthroughs in history have at first been labeled "mistakes" (vulcanization of rubber, the x-ray, drilling for water, and discovering oil), so I value my mistakes in terms of what they can contribute to my new knowledge.

Non-Questions:

"Why" Daggers

Have You Noticed Your Boss Repeatedly Stabbing You with "Why" Questions Without Really Expecting Answers?

(See Chapter 3, Signature Pattern No. 6, Numbing.)
(See Chapter 4, Game No. 3, Heads I Win, Tails You Lose.)

Dragons and Doorkeepers typically gang up on victims using a barrage of questions involving "*why*" and "*you*." We will begin by looking carefully at the "why" dagger. When an abuser asks "why" in an intimidating voice, there is never a correct answer. No matter how the employee responds, the answer is always judged to be wrong, stupid, and thoughtless. In fact, "why" from a Dragon is not a question; it is almost always a *put-down*. It is a game that powerful bullies enjoy: a verbal contest, a victory that the victim can never win, and a dagger aimed directly at the victim's self-esteem.

> Beth, the Director of Training for a wholesale food company, was to set up staff training on the new computer system being installed. Although Beth did not yet know that she had been set up for failure to create a case for dismissal, she had learned to walk on eggshells. She consulted

her boss for specific instructions on how he wanted the training handled. His response was, "Do it the way you want. After all, that's your job. Just do it right!"

Beth took him at his word, setting up the program agendas and the time schedule for evening classes. Her Dragon raged, "WHY didn't you set up the classes in the morning? What a stupid move! Now the employees will want overtime!"

Beth replied that training sessions in the morning would not allow enough time for employees to ask questions of the trainer. The boss yelled, "If the dummies have to ask questions, then the instruction is not good enough." He followed up with a letter of reprimand pointing out her inadequate planning.

There is a sequel to this story. Several employees told the boss how good it was to have the class in the early evening because it gave everyone time to relax, to ask questions, and to get extra hands-on practice with the new computers. Having no idea that the boss had just reprimanded Beth for poor planning, they went to praise her for her insightful planning attuned to their specific needs. The Dragon smiled, thanked the staff members, and left. The next morning, he called Beth into his office and shouted, "WHY?"

"Why did you talk about me behind my back? Why did you solicit support for yourself from other staff members? Why did you pick that presenter? It is obvious that you picked the poorest instructor and did the poorest planning if the staff had to ask all kinds of questions and needed extra practice time. In the future, you had better select someone who knows how to teach and be discreet about what you say!"

He followed up with another letter of reprimand to Beth, who was by then a very bewildered Director of Staff Training. This is another case where the victim is a threat to the Dragon because of the boss's poor knowledge of company operations. Note how the Dragon accused Beth of talking behind his back in addition to other accusations. He used the *lie* to cause still more pain and confusion.

Just as in Beth's case, sometimes clients unwittingly play into a Dragon's hand when they call a supervisor to express thanks for special problem-solving assistance given by an employee who the Dragon is currently victimizing. When the client calls to praise a victim concerning a job that was well done, the Dragon will act interested and may even take credit for the victim's planning and actions. The boss will ask in-depth questions of the client concerning what occurred. Having usurped the victim's just reward, the abuser will again attack the victim with the "why" dagger. The boss will ask questions that range from "Why did you spend so much time with this client?" to "Why did this problem exist in the first place?"

If you have heard *"why this"* and *"why that"* and no answer seems to be appropriate, an attempt is possibly being made to keep you bewildered. In that state, you are likely to remain unable to understand what needs to be done at work and what you are actually accomplishing.

Dragon Smoke

Irrational thoughts that the Dragon wants you to think:

Every question has an answer. There are right answers and wrong answers. I must answer the question correctly or I am stupid. If I am confused, it is my fault. I should always be able to come up with perfect explanations about everything my boss asks. Perfect answers are those that agree with the boss's logic. The boss is logical. Therefore, if I do not have the same answers as the boss, I must be illogical. I am confused. Confused employees are not good for the company. I must not be a good employee or I would know what I am doing.

Dragon-Taming Thoughts

Rational replacement thoughts:

The "why" question is not really a question and has no correct answer. It is simply a power play designed to criticize, intimidate, and put me on the defensive. Any answer makes me a loser. I can choose not to play the game by doing the opposite of what is expected. Rather than try to answer a non-question or become defensive, I can simply sidestep the issue with answers like: "That's a good question. I will certainly give it some serious thought," or "I'm wondering why, too."

Then I can use my own personal power to bounce the question back with statements like: "I'm really interested in your ideas. Do you have any thoughts about why?" Then, I will step back emotionally and wait for a barrage of critical remarks. I realize that I have deliberately put the Dragon on the defensive. I have stepped on the Dragon's tail. I will not take the remarks personally; they only reveal the boss's logic (or lack of it).

Dragon-Proofing Beliefs

I am capable. I can answer questions that are genuine, but I can also detect those that are non-questions. I can choose how to respond. I can sift through criticism and decide for myself how much is genuine and how much is simply a Dragon's smoke.

Comments

The "why" dagger seems to be a rational question until you recognize it is merely a power game. It evokes emotions that put you, the victim, in a subordinate position.

Apparently you are doing things so well that the Dragon is becoming nervous enough to stoop to such intimidation. Congratulate yourself but take note of any justifiable criticisms. Check them out later to be sure that you are not overlooking something that will help you cope with your Dragon.

"You" Guns

Now that You Understand the Point of the "Why" Dagger, Can You Recognize Being Hit with the "You" Gun?

(See Chapter 3, Signature Pattern No. 6, Numbing and Nullifying.)
(See Chapter 4, Game No. 5, Blame and Shame, That's Our Game.)

Dragons are skilled at being verbally abusive, and the "you" gun is another one of their favorite weapons. The "you" gun is a psychological finger of blame pointed directly at your emotions. Angry and/or subtle "you" statements are intended to destroy your confidence and your ability to deal rationally with your fears. Notice that some common "you" guns include "why" as well:

1. Why did YOU do ...
2. Why didn't YOU think about ...
3. Why don't YOU ever get this right . . .
4. Why didn't YOU follow my instructions . . .
5. YOU stupid so and so . . .
6. YOU are failing . . .
7. YOU should have . . .
8. YOU should not have . . .
9. YOU'LL never get this right . . .
10. YOU are worthless . . .

11. YOU never keep your word . . .
12. YOU never understand . . .
13. YOU had better do this right . . .
14. Why do YOU have to be different . . .
15. YOU freak me out . . .
16. YOU didn't listen to . . .
17. YOU are putting the company at risk . . .
18. Why are YOU trying to get me in trouble with . . .
19. YOU know better . . .
20. YOU should have known better . . .
21. Why are YOU going to school? YOU are overeducated as it is!
22. YOU are overpaid . . . overqualified . . .
23. YOU are undereducated . . . underqualified . . .

The list goes on and on. At first each of these bullets may appear to be justified or painless, but with enough use of these weapons, a Dragon can confuse you and undermine your self-confidence. In the beginning, time intervals between blasts from the "you" gun are relatively far apart. After enough of these psychological bullets have found their mark, however, you might become immobilized and/or depressed.

"Hit them when they're down" is a common Dragon motto. The "you" gun tends to be fired off with ever increasing frequency and effect. However, when an intended victim becomes wise to the power play, the use of *"why"* and *"you"* becomes rather ridiculous and humorous.

A computer technician, Mark, who was working under a new and abusive boss, was met with a barrage of questions and mind-twisting comments such as:

- WHY are YOU trying to avoid me?
- Don't YOU ever stop to see me!
- I get the feeling that YOU are afraid of me.
- WHY don't YOU answer my phone calls? (In reality, Mark did answer the calls. It was the Dragon that didn't answer Mark's calls.)
- YOU better keep me informed.
- YOUR management style is lacking. People have no respect for YOU.

These statements increased in frequency so that finally Mark said that all he wanted to do was quit.

In an effort to deflect the "you" bullets, some employees try to explain why indeed they did (or did not) do what the boss claims. They are then shocked when the most lucid and logical explanations fall on deaf ears. The Dragon proves to be neither capable of understanding their reasoning nor caring about the action that they were defending. Remember that "why" is never a question but an *attempt at intimidation and manipulation* when the boss is a Dragon.

Dragon Smoke

Irrational thoughts that the boss wants you to think:

I am trying to hear what the boss is saying. I feel like a child with a huge finger of blame being pointed at my nose. I am helpless, blocked, and speechless. No matter what I say, the boss does not hear me, and I come off as defensive about things I have never even done. Maybe if I do not say anything, these problems will stop. I am powerless. Let me out of here! I had better not slam the door when I leave. I hope the boss calms down soon. If I put in more hours and do better work, maybe I will be liked. If the boss doesn't like me, I could lose my job.

Dragon-Taming Thoughts

Rational replacement thoughts:

This conversation is just another of the Dragon's power plays. This one is easy to handle now that I know the key words *"why" and "you."* They jump out of the boss's tirade, letting me know that none of these questions has an answer and that no rational, accurate answers are acceptable. The boss simply wants to show power. When the boss is through having a tantrum, I will be ready to say, "I hear you." It is amazing how someone with that position in the company can use such foolish techniques as a simple little "you" gun. The boss is telling me much more than is suspected. When I say, "Yes, I hear you," I mean it. I hear far more than the boss thinks. The message is not about me. When I am called a fool, the boss is actually displaying a personal pathology and unsuitability. The boss is displaying self-doubt.

Dragon-Proofing Beliefs

I am growing stronger every day. I realize that we humans are incredibly capable of handling stress and that understanding what is going on is an excellent way to deal with the feelings that I am having. Now that I understand the "you" gun, I am free from knee-jerk responses and can simply wait out the tirade and choose my responses calmly and rationally.

Comments

For most people who are in therapy for work-related abuse issues, the first concrete example of a "tolerable" Dragon tirade is that which includes the *"why"* and the *"you"* weapons. At this point, most clients seem to gain insight. They begin to change their responses to the Dragon's intimidation. They begin to break away from fearful self-doubts such as:

- Will I lose my job?
- Am I going to be unemployed and homeless?
- What can I do?
- Where can I turn?

They turn instead toward a sense of personal power. They begin to see the Dragon tracks, recognize the power games, and regain their sense of self-control. Psychological movement typically begins with recognizing these ploys and then gains more strength each day. Soon they can put their lives back together and their careers back on track.

Summary

There are a variety of extinguishers that are useful against Dragon fire and smoke. The most important of these is staying alert and aware. Spot the pressure ploys and fight mystification by checking out reality. Understand that when a Dragon attacks you, your belief system is under attack. When pressured, block the Dragon's fire by hanging on to your own basic beliefs. You can Dragon-proof yourself against further abuse by making your own decisions and taking charge of your life. The process of disarming Dragons is summarized below in the grid with the four labels: Dragon Fire, Dragon Smoke, Dragon Taming, and Dragon Proofing.

Disarming Dragons Table 9-1

	Example A	*Example B*
Dragon Fire *Brainwashing:* What the Dragon does to gain confidence and exert power and control over another. *Victimization:* Grooming, The Setup, the Hook	"You aren't sexy enough to make it here. You better go out with me tonight – and show a little skin if you want a real bonus this year."	"Sign your name just as though you had received the package."
Dragon Smoke *Mystification:* Confusing and then attacking victims' beliefs and ethics. What the Dragon wants me to think in order to gain power over me.	The Dragon wants me to believe that dating and being sexy lead to a big bonus. (Confusion: does that mean no sex, no bonus?)	The Dragon wants me to think that it is okay to steal from the company if ordered to do so by the boss.
Dragon Taming *Resistance*: Self-talk to disarm the Dragon fire and smoke; how I am interpreting my experiences in light of my ethics.	I recognize the Dragon smoke and "you" gun. I am being pressured to compromise my values.	I know it is wrong to take things, even if the boss tells me to do it.
Dragon Proofing *Recovery:* Information, thoughts, and acts that protect personal power, freedom, and integrity from victimization and bullying.	I know what is right or wrong for me. I will make my own decisions and guard against "grooming."	I am not willing to front for theft. It may be a setup or a misunderstanding. I will question this and get the order in writing.

Practice Disarming Dragons Table 9-2

Practice disarming Dragons with your own fire extinguishing skills. Fill in the blanks below with your own experiences.

Dragon Fire
The situation was:

Dragon Smoke
My irrational thoughts were:

Dragon Taming
My replacement thoughts are:

Dragon Proofing
My Dragon-proofing action plans are:

Chapter 10

Subtle Abuse

Punishing yourself for something that you are not responsible for is illogical; yet, it seems that we always try to make sense out of the senseless. Like the battered spouse, even though we know the boss is a Dragon, we are quick to attribute negative attitudes to some personal fault in ourselves. Regardless of what you say or do or how hard you work, nothing seems to change. The longer you stay in a dysfunctional workplace, the more abused and powerless you will feel. Once you clearly recognize the Dragon tracks, you can focus your energy on changing things. Understanding that you have been selected for abuse gives you personal power. You can take positive actions against the boss's subtle mind games that are aimed at getting you to blame and punish yourself.

The challenging part is spotting the abuse of power when it occurs. Subtle abuse disguised as simply "*doing business*" mystifies us. It typically ranges from crude remarks to borderline criminal behavior. The most common forms of subtle abuse in the workplace include:

- *Discrimination* (See Chapter 3, Signature Pattern No. 2, Relationships.)
- *Isolation* (See Chapter 3, Signature Pattern No. 5, Ostracizing.)
- *Economic abuse* (See Chapter 3, Signature Pattern No. 4, Grooming.)
- *Increased workload* (See Chapter 3, Signature Pattern No. 6, Numbing, and Chapter 4, Game No. 6, the Rumpelstiltskin Ploy.)

Dragons are devious, not stupid. They are likely to avoid public demonstration of the obvious issues (gender, age, race, and physical disability) that may land them in court. They save the direct and dirty attacks for the private "motivational" talks where "your word against mine" manipulations assure victory for them.

Do any of these circumstances seem familiar to you?

- You are slowly being isolated from other staff members or the power group. (See Chapter 3, Signature Pattern No. 5, Ostracizing and Chapter 4, Game No. 2, Divide and Conquer.)
- You are deprived of positive comments. (See Chapter 3, Signature Pattern No. 4, Grooming and Chapter 4, Game No. 5, Blame and Shame.)
- You are denied the information and the financial support necessary for success on the job. (See Chapter 3, Signature Pattern No. 4, Grooming and Chapter 4, Game No. 1, Blind Man's Bluff.)

If any of these scenarios are occurring, you might be a victim of the most common of the Dragon's subtle, discriminatory abuse patterns, especially if your workload has also increased exponentially. (See Chapter 3, Signature Pattern No. 6, Numbing and Nullifying and Chapter 4, Game No. 6, the Rumpelstiltskin Ploy.) The ultimate goal of the abuser is to set you up for failure and dismissal.

> Arnold was a middle-management officer who came up through the ranks. He achieved his master's degree in business administration through the firm's educational plan. He was, however, subjected to discrimination when the company's atmosphere suddenly changed dramatically.
>
> A new CEO, a Dragon and former athlete, began his new position with the typical Dragon ploy of restructuring the organization to be "lean, mean, and competitive." He implemented a cost-reduction plan of eliminating the highest paid positions and replacing some of them with less expensive employees. His own handsome salary, of course, was an exception. His hit list included Arnold and others

who expressed concerns and asked questions. They were the employees who were most knowledgeable about customer needs and services.

The new company focus was to be on sales and marketing. Although the new policy never stated it openly, one additional requirement for all new replacements was that they needed to have strong athletic records. Athletes with advanced degrees, however, were eliminated. New competitive sales teams were pitted against one another as commissions and bonuses replaced more worthwhile goals of customers' needs and service, product development, and quality control.

As Doorkeepers were groomed, the subtle discrimination took its toll. Retirements and resignations increased rapidly, and employee morale dropped as budgets for customer service and research were cut. Revenues began to fall, which created more obvious reasons for the company to save money by downsizing. Meanwhile, Arnold could not simply be fired. He was too respected by employees and customers. He had a detailed understanding of the company's workforce and customer needs. The Dragon decided that the most effective way to victimize Arnold was through subtle discrimination aimed at exploiting his knowledge while coaxing him to resign.

This is what makes the attacks on excellent people so difficult to understand. On the one hand, the victims are used for their knowledge levels, but at the same time, they are set up for failure. Arnold's company had taken a giant step backward. In today's competitive market, concerns for customer needs, service, and employee morale are correctly recognized as significant factors to maintain corporate health. The manipulator's false budgeting was eventually found to be Dragon smoke: misleading, unnecessary, and eventually destructive. One of the earliest reductions, the employee-training budget, was reallocated for executive travel, with pseudo-training vacations for the CEO and Doorkeepers in exotic settings. The competition between sales representatives inflated the costs of advertising and sales.

The new CEO collected generous bonuses for his downsizing and apparent innovations. These "innovations" included the dismissals of people for their alleged harm to the company who were, in reality, threats to the Dragon. This company regressed in the hands of a tyrant who tried to lower it to the level of an athletic game. He understood only trumped-up, interdependent competition and the abuse of power to produce short-term, artificial gains. Examples of such subtle abuse tactics include usurping ideas, taking credit for someone else's work, isolation, and economic abuse.

Usurping

(See Chapter 3, Signature Pattern No. 6, Numbing.)

Just as a black widow drains her mate for her own purposes, the Dragon has reasons for designating certain victims as a slow banquet rather than fast food for immediate dismissal. Although victims are perceived as threats, the Dragon needs their knowledge and therefore, operates under the premise of "what's yours is mine." It is a covert operation that drains victims of their creativity, patents, ideas, and royalties by:

- Taking personal credit for the employee's accomplishments without giving any credit to the employee.
- Asking for ideas and then using them with no recognition for the originator.
- Giving employees a private thank you but accepting credit for the work in public as the Dragon's own.
- Accepting royalties for an idea that someone else suggested to the Dragon.
- When the department does well because of employee suggestions, the Dragon takes all the credit as the supervisor without mentioning the source.

One manufacturing company offered to pay $1,000 for any employee's suggestion instituted in its final form. The company used many suggestions without paying anything because they modified the applications of the suggestions slightly from how the suggestions were worded by the employees. The result was that employees stopped giving suggestions, but no one recognized the Dragon mentality.

A positive story comes from an aircraft company who published the names of each employee who made suggestions in its monthly magazine and paid out bonuses monthly. They made no effort to hide the source of suggestions. Consequently, suggestion-giving improved. No Dragon took the credit!

Under a Dragon's control, it is not unusual for research to be credited to the department heads and superintendents rather than to the researcher. Unfortunately, such usurping goes on in many organizations at all levels.

Isolation

(See Chapter 3, Signature Pattern No. 5, Ostracizing.)

- Are you being isolated or moved into a different group?
- Are cliques forming in your workplace?
- Have you found yourself shut out of the group with which you were previously associated?
- Does your group have less access to the boss and get less information and necessary equipment than others do?
- Is it puzzling that you and some of your fellow "isolates" are among the best employees?

If other employees sense that you are slated for removal and fear that they may be next, they might pull away from you. Coworkers know that you are a good employee, but it is natural for them to want to protect their own careers. Ignoring your plight may seem like the safest way to protect themselves. If you are successfully eliminated from the company, some of these people will discover that their chosen avenue was not so wise after all. They could be the next Dragon snack. An abuser must always have a victim, and when one is gone, another is needed.

Friendships are at risk in an abusive workplace. You and your coworkers may have shared problems, jokes, and light bantering in the past. When a Dragon is in power, however, these friendships come under suspicion. An atmosphere that was once conducive to creativity and hard work becomes heavy and depressing. You are apt to feel a very real sense of rejection as some of your fellow employees pull away from you. You might also pull away from them and from others on the job, in your community, and even at home. The Dragon's objective is to isolate you from support and from the flow of helpful information necessary for positive job performance.

You and your fellow "isolates" may have gone on record as being interested in producing a quality product, saving money for the company, and building positive relationships with the customers. Surprise! Dragons are not interested in any of these things, although they will give them lip service. Successes in these areas are threatening to Dragons. They will try to disable or remove you before you do anything that merits intense, positive attention. The following is an example of just how negative a Dragon can be regarding positive work and customer relations.

> Reggie visited with two or three customers per day, talking with them about their needs. Because of his approach, he eventually achieved first place in sales within his first two years on the job. Reggie's supervisor became

quite jealous, not only because of Reggie's sales success but also because of his close working relationships with customers. The intimidated Doorkeepers complained to the Dragon that Reggie was not achieving the suggested customer-contact quota of six (or more) per day.

The Dragon was furious with Reggie. In a private meeting, he told Reggie that attaining the highest sales level was just fine but that he could be doing so much more for the company if he visited the recommended number of customers every day. Reggie tried to explain why his system of customer relations worked so well, but the Dragon would not listen. He ordered Reggie to increase the number of customer visits or else. Reggie tried to increase his frequency of contacts, but he immediately detected a slippage in sales. He went back to his customary method that had earned him first place.

Customers began to detect a decrease in energy and some evidence of depression in Reggie. Some even tried to cheer him up a bit. An interesting twist to this story began when a group of customers called Reggie's boss to express their gratitude about what a terrific job Reggie was doing for them. Jealous of the support Reggie was receiving from the customers, the Dragon thanked them profusely and then called Reggie in for another scream session.

Reggie was transferred from his sales position to a number crunching "desk job" just outside the Dragon's office. Placed right under the Dragon's nose, Reggie experienced the ultimate in isolation. Meanwhile, sales dropped for the company in Reggie's territory. The Dragon explained the loss as a *temporary correction* in the marketplace, a classic example of an *effective lie* often used by abusive supervisors.

People are astounded by this story. A typical response is, "No marketing manager would ever do that!" You must keep in mind, however, that the Dragon cares not for the company. Dragons are driven by their insatiable need to satisfy their lust for power and control. A top sales person with public support is no longer vulnerable to a single Dragon and, therefore, is out of control.

An honest supervisor delights in having employees who are highly skilled and well liked by their customers. They are never reluctant to employ and reward these people. Unfortunately, as mentioned several times before, such employees are threats to Dragons. Dragons favor employing people who they believe are inferior and are therefore easily controlled or can be used to do the dirty work. If your boss is a Dragon and you are being taken out of the "loop," then you know that you are a skilled employee doing an excellent job. Congratulations!

Economic Abuse

(See Chapter 3, Signature Pattern No. 2, Relationships.)

If any of the following statements describes your situation, you might be a victim of economic abuse.

- Has your salary been reduced?
- Have you been denied a raise in salary that you deserved?
- Have even less deserving employees received pay raises?
- Was your department's budget cut?
- Have items previously allowed on an expense account been taken from you?

A Dragon had targeted a highly talented, middle-level supervisor, Emily, for dismissal. He cut the department budget so that it would become more difficult for Emily to carry out the duties of the department. She set up an appointment with Bob, the Dragon.

Emily: Quite frankly Bob, my budget allocations are not going to permit us to carry out our required duties and production.

Bob: That's just the way it is Emily. You'll just have to make do!

Emily: But it certainly appears that your budget allocation is bigger than last year.

Bob: We are not talking about my budget; we are talking about yours. If you cannot do the job, we will find someone who can.

Notice the threats and the evasiveness in the conversation. The Dragon does not provide any logical explanations for the budget reduction because there are none.

Economic abuse serves several purposes for the Dragon:

- It gives senior management the impression that the supervisor (Dragon) knows how to reduce costs effectively.
- By cutting your budget, the Dragon ensures that you will not be able to do your job as effectively as you have in the past.
- If your income has been reduced, the Dragon is now able to attack your personal life and well-being.

It is especially important to document the effect that the financial cuts have made on your department and on your performance. If you are asked why you have not done as complete a job as in the past, produce proof of the impact that this funding loss has had on your department.

Is Your Boss Piling On the Work While Depriving You of Positive Feedback?

(See Chapter 4, Game No. 6, the Rumpelstiltskin Ploy.)

In a deliberate effort to harm an employee, an abusive boss will pile on more and more work, steadily increasing expectations. At the same time, the Dragon will not, in any way, acknowledge the successes of the victim. It is discouraging and frustrating to try to do a complete job when the workload becomes too large and contains too varied an array of assignments. Dragons may accomplish this pressure-cooker effect by transferring an employee to another job, changing job descriptions, or by simply increasing demands until the victim is too weary to put up any more resistance. The victim has become Dragon food!

When a Dragon *piles it on,* most people attempt to discuss the problem with the boss. However, such a discussion creates an opportunity for the Dragon to assign blame or fly into a rage, and it tends to make the victim feel even more inadequate. When objections are raised, typical Dragon responses include:

- "I don't know what your problem is. Everybody else is doing the same amount of work."
- "Where have you been? Everyone else understands! When are you going to catch on that everyone must now do more with less?"
- "If you cannot do it, we will get somebody who can. You had better not forget what I said. We can replace you in a blink of an eye."
- "If you can't stand the heat, get out of the kitchen. We do not need complaining jerks like you around here. Now get to work!"

- "You say you had to work last night? That means you can't even budget your time. If that's the case, we will get someone who can tell time."

- "So you need another secretary? You're not really using the one you have. Don't be so nice!"

Dragons like to pile on discouragement. Triple binds discourage even more effectively than double binds. Sometimes a Dragon will take a project that has been discarded, undermined, or even turned down in the past and assign it to a victim. This project has no chance of succeeding, and everyone but the victim knows it.

1. If the victim succeeds in launching the project, the Dragon will explode because the boss never wanted it to succeed. The abuser's next move would be to add the new project to the victim's regular workload without extra resources or compensation.

2. If the employee recommends dropping the project, the Dragon refuses to consider the recommendation.

3. If the victim fails with the project, the Dragon cites this failure as a reason to abuse, demote, or fire the victim.

Questions to consider:

- Has your job description been changed under the guise of either increased responsibility or restructuring?

- Are you working harder than ever but not feeling rewarded?

- Have you lost satisfaction in the work that you are doing and feel discouraged about your job?

Take a careful look at your workload. Ask yourself, "What was expected of me before my new boss arrived?" Check to see if your workload has been increasing in small increments. Remember that there are times when all organizations must provide more services with less revenue. Your task is to determine whether or not your boss's demands are legitimate and within expectancy limits or way over the line and discriminatory.

Are you running around in circles trying to please a Dragon while fearing that you will never be able to do so? You are probably right! Dragons are never satisfied. In fact, your failure is the only thing that will please a Dragon. If you did succeed in accomplishing the impossible, completing every assignment within the required time and on budget, an honest boss would be delighted. A Dragon boss, however, would be furious because accomplishing assignments is not the Dragon's goal. Abuse of power, abuse of you, and abuse of the system are what the Dragon feeds upon. Calm down and do the best you can but take care of yourself in the process.

Dragon Smoke

Irrational thoughts that the Dragon wants you to have:

I do not know what is going on, but I am feeling stressed out and confused lately. It seems that I cannot keep up with all the work coming my way. I have trouble remembering all the things I am supposed to do.

The boss says that I am forgetful, that I should know certain pieces of information that I do not remember having received. Other times, when I am absolutely sure that I do not have the desired information, the boss points out, "You know (or you should be responsible for knowing) that I want this...." I am puzzled by my own thoughts lately. When I ask for more explicit directions, I feel like a fool. I run into my boss's anger no matter what I do. I am so embarrassed when I make the boss mad and get called names and ridiculed. The boss is probably as stressed out as I am. I will stay out of the way and just work harder.

Some of the others in the office seem to get their memos in a timely manner, so I depend on asking them when I need help. They seem to be pulling away from me lately. I wonder if they don't like me either. The boss does not call them names all the time, so it must be me. I am lucky to have this job, but I get so nervous when I am supervised that I can hardly concentrate. I guess I had better work harder – come in on weekends to make up the work I cannot finish and then do a little bit more. I hope I can please the boss.

I will do anything to keep my job, but now I have to produce the same results with about half the budget that I had last year. Maybe I could volunteer to take a cut in my pay. It will be tough, but I will do whatever the boss says. I know I will not be getting a raise this year or any time in the future, but others in the department will. I guess that I just don't measure up.

I am spinning my wheels. I must go to a doctor and get something for my nerves so that I can sleep at night. Then perhaps I can think clearly and perform more effectively.

Dragon-Taming Thoughts

Rational replacement thoughts:

I am feeling stressed and confused about my job, so I think that I will document my feelings about what has been going on in my DD. I will make a list of abuses that I have noticed.

Subtle Abuse Checklist:

1. *Discrimination*	The boss calls me names with a barrage of put-downs and ridicule. Even the insiders badger me with his consent.
2. *Isolation*	I do not get my memos but insiders do. I am blamed for not having memos on time. Others pull away from me when I ask for help.
3. *Economic Abuse*	My budget has decreased while insiders got increases.
4. *Increased Workload*	My workload has greatly increased this year, more so than some others!

Conclusion

I have spotted some subtle discrimination. I am feeling stress, but I am no longer confused. I am angry. I do not need a doctor. Instead I will consider my options, make some decisions, and take some action. I will use the energy and determination from my anger to get on with my life. Now I can focus on the problem of dealing with subtle abuse and discrimination.

Dragon-Proofing Beliefs

I believe in myself. I can take stress when I can focus on it. I know that anyone subjected to discrimination has the right to speak up about it. I am entitled to direct answers about information, budgets, and my increased workload. I believe that it is only fair to confront my boss about the ridicule. I have the right to tell him how I feel and how his comments have affected my performance. I will request that the put-downs end! I have the right to discuss my feelings in private conversations with my coworkers. It is okay to ask them about specific incidents when I feel unfairly isolated.

Discussion: Keys to Disarming Dragons

Being subjected to subtle discrimination is unfair but unfortunately not criminal. In fact, it is a common practice among employers who want to set up employees for dismissal. If employers avoid the obvious legal discrimination issues, as well as the name calling, they are successful. They keep up the pressure until the employee leaves without a confrontation and without realizing that the employer has created the dismissal. By keeping the victim in the dark but increasing the pressures, many manipulative employers actually make their employees ill. When attendance and productivity suffer, these victims can simply be dismissed for inefficiency.

If you believe that your boss is a Dragon and you spot subtle abusive maneuvers, document and date everything. If you decide to confront your boss, be ready to receive a personal attack instead of genuine answers. Such a response from your boss, while unpleasant, is proof positive that your suspicions are correct. Let's try the following *exercise.*

Be Prepared

Now that you have a name for each of the typical offenses, decide which issue is bothering you. Using your DD, write out specific questions that you intend to ask your boss and leave space for answers. For example, the questions you formulate to put in your DD might go like this:

1. Information Control

I have noticed that I do not receive your memos in a timely fashion. For example, the memo about the meeting on October 8th at 7:00 a.m. did not reach my desk until October 10th. By missing that meeting, I was denied my vote on the John Doe tenure decision. On September 15th, I was the only one in my department who did not receive your notice about deadlines for budgetary considerations. I was not prepared for the meeting on the 16th and was reprimanded for my *inefficiency*. Can you help me understand where the problem lies, and what I can do about seeing to it that important memos reach my desk? Is there something you can do to resolve this problem with me?

2. Budget

My budget has been cut again while my workload has increased. Will you please show me where and why these changes have been made? What is the rationale? Will you share your expertise with me? What, specifically, can I do to complete the job specifications within the new budget restrictions?

3. Workload

Here is my list of duties, along with a daily log and time sheet to show you what I am presently doing. As I contrast this to my workload last month, I can see that a significant change has occurred. I have compared my present duties with those of Jane Doe. Although we have the same titles and job descriptions, your expectations for me are significantly higher when I compare them to my own records or to Jane's. Can you help me to understand your rationale?

4. Ridicule

I want you to know when I make a mistake or when I need corrective information that I am certainly willing to give your words serious consideration and make whatever changes you feel are necessary. After all, you are the boss. It is not what is said, but how it is said that bothers me. I do not like to be degraded or called names. I consider ridicule abusive, and I am not willing to endure it. Please consider my feelings, just as I consider your dignity and respect your position as my boss.

Now that you are prepared with a topic that you want to discuss and the points that you wish to address, make an appointment with your boss. Discuss one concern, and be specific. Do not use all of your grievances in a shotgun approach. For example, if your concern is information control, pick a specific example of when, where, and how you experienced a problem with information control. Be ready to use the questions you have prepared in your DD during the meeting but resist the urge to move on to other issues, such as discrimination, budget, or workload. (See Chapter 12, Test the Boss.)

Back to Your Dragon Diary

Do not forget to document the results in your DD. Be as objective as possible.

- Were you able to meet with the boss?
- Were you able to stick to one major issue?
- Were you able to present your grievances in question form as you had planned?
- Were you attacked?
- What was the outcome?
- How do you feel?

Leave space for long-term as well as short-term results of your efforts to confront subtle abuse with assertive action in your workplace.

Chapter 11

Deliberate Abuse

Are You Being Forced Out?

When subtle discrimination becomes deliberate and suggestions turn to harassment, you are being forced out. If you are targeted for dismissal, and it is taking longer to get rid of you than planned, subtle abuse becomes deliberate and obvious. Victims sometimes even deny blatant abuse, especially if they have been hooked by the subtle brainwashing techniques. In some workplaces, the abuse involves fear induced by blackmail, injury, and extreme intimidation. In other situations, the abuse of power is *polite* but just as intimidating and just as obvious. The fear of losing your job, security, perks, or reputation can be devastating. For some, it is terrorizing and debilitating. For others, who are beginning to understand the mystification process, the fear and anger motivates action whereby victims begin taking charge of their lives and reclaiming their freedom.

What About Sexual Harassment?

(See Chapter 3, Signature Pattern No. 2, Relationships.)

Typical Dragons feel as though they have the right to force employees into subordinate roles. This real or imagined power allows them to assume that they have the right to abuse and harass employees sexually, and they often attempt to hold sexual power over victims. Sexual power often plays a big role in inflating the warped ego of a Dragon. While laws provide some protection for the victims, many people are so vulnerable that they are afraid to report such treatment. Both men and women can be victimized in this manner, and Dragons can be especially vicious when their attempts to wield power and control by their sexual demands are thwarted.

There is often misunderstanding among people about exactly where the line is drawn between "friendly" persuasion and harassment. A direct threat of *"sex or else"* is probably the crudest form of sexual harassment and has rapidly left the workplace as current court cases sound their warnings. Direct threats are now often avoided by Dragons, making it all the more difficult for victims to prove their cases.

One woman reported that her Dragon boss never made a "specific request" for sex but made many subtle actions and comments with a variety of tones that indicated what he wanted. Many Dragons will deny that there was any sexual intent but do have the grandiose delusion that it is perfectly permissible to continue harassing and intimidating their victims long after it is believed that the word "no" has been heard. What might a victim of sexual harassment think?

Dragon Smoke

Irrational thoughts that the boss wants me to think:

The boss is so powerful and so respected that no one would believe my story. I can't say "no" and keep my job here. I should be happy I have my job and be quiet about any suggestive innuendoes. Otherwise, my future is in jeopardy. I should be flattered with the references to my attractiveness and sexuality. My boss is just trying to show me how to get ahead. If we have an affair, I could be guaranteed a successful career with all the advancements that I want. Perhaps the boss is in love with me and we will be married; then I will have it all.

Dragon-Taming Thoughts

Rational replacement thoughts:

Name-calling, teasing, gruffness, nonverbal actions, and a suggestive tone of voice are all power plays aimed toward me, attempting to override my "no." These activities tell me that my future in this position includes innuendoes and pressures that are unacceptable. Therefore, I must speak up. I must be clear about my position that these are unacceptable behaviors and ask for what I want. I will secure a positive recommendation and move on if things do not change.

Dragon-Proofing Beliefs

I have integrity, and I am not willing to compromise my values for a job. My identity does not lie in my career title. I have courage. I have choices. I am free to do what I think is best for me. Negative pressures from my boss are contributing to my health problems, so I must see that those pressures stop or I must leave. I have the right to file a complaint and to sue if I have been sexually harassed and forced from my job.

Comments

Sexual harassment involves repeated demands for sex, unwanted physical contact, explicit remarks disguised as jokes, comments about body parts, exposure to obscene pictures, or any continued actions that cause the victim to feel uncomfortable. Learn to recognize harassment for what it is, a part of the grooming process for either becoming one of the Dragon's group or becoming one of the victims. Do not ever give silent approval to such actions and then later shout harassment. Respond immediately; speak up about your values and be assertive about your intent to have such behaviors cease immediately. Document all incidents in your DD. If the harassment continues, put physical space between you and the abuser. Seek assistance. Remember, sexual harassment of any sort is illegal. You do not have to tolerate it, not even to save your job.

Letters of Reprimand

(See Chapter 4, Game No. 6, The Rumpelstiltskin Ploy.)

Do your supervisory letters turn negative and contain broad, general remarks such as, "We do not expect you to succeed," or "I am concerned about your ability to respond to our expectations?"

Are they followed by a flurry of memos containing various negative comments? Are they supplemented by summaries of previous negative comments, along with demands for improved quality, quantity, and attitude? If any of these questions can be answered affirmatively, your boss may be playing the Rumpelstiltskin game.

If these communications are from a Dragon, their purpose is probably to "unnerve" you, to create extreme stress and add mountains of work to your load. The Dragon wants to stimulate emotions in you such as anger, fear, depression, and the desire to leave. If the dirty tricks accomplish their purpose, your performance will deteriorate. The Dragon boss will at last have an excuse (your poor performance) to send a reprimand and terminate your employment.

Dragon Smoke

Irrational thoughts that the Dragon wants you to think:

I am so stupid that I cannot even remember all the things on my job description. Here it is in black and white. I am a failure. I cannot live up to my boss' expectations. I guess that I am lucky to have any job at all. I do not think that these expectations are fair, but the boss is the one I need to please. I am helpless and hopeless, so I will just quietly quit and go away.

Dragon-Taming Thoughts

Rational replacement thoughts:

I recognize this paper flurry as the Rumpelstiltskin ploy, a technique to confuse me and create the appearance of mistakes when I am not actually making any. My boss is demanding that I spin straw into gold and will attack me when I fail. I can keep my emotions under control by knowing the rules of the game. I can carefully document everything, making sure that I *get it in writing* whenever I am observed or supervised. I can do my best while handling my stress levels with self-talk like this:

- I must certainly be a threat to my boss. I am probably thought of as superior to the boss in some way.
- I must be doing my job well. Otherwise, such a paper flurry would not be necessary. Legitimate documentation should be enough to show my mistakes. Then I could correct them.
- I am keeping my attention on my work and doing my best.
- I am focusing on customer service as well as my own goals, while even trying to accommodate the increased workload.
- What a workout! And I'm feeling great! Is this stress or what? I feel like I'm running a marathon!
- I am documenting everything. It is great to realize how much I actually do every day!
- It is amazing how much energy I have now that it is focused and I am not confused about the Rumpelstiltskin ploy.

Dragon-Proofing Beliefs

I have the personal power to handle stress physically and emotionally. I am good to myself and am watching my diet, blood pressure, and exercise. I can choose whether or not I wish to stay or to leave. I enjoy my power and am glad I do not need to victimize anybody. I am never helpless as long as I am doing my best on the job. I am saving all paper correspondence, writing in my journal, and documenting everything while considering my many options. I am never without choices.

Tormenting the Victim

(See Chapter 3, Signature Pattern No. 2, Relationships.)

In addition to obvious harassment, Dragons sometimes create negative employee history files and manufacture evidence to support unfair dismissals. They typically ignore all positive information, issue unwarranted disciplinary write-ups, and subject the individual to transfers that were not requested.

There have been cases reported to us where individuals have made a request to examine their personnel files and found letters of reprimand that they never received and investigations of negative incidents that never took place. Many organizations have a policy stating that employees who wish to look at their files must make a written request several days (or even a month) in advance. This provides the Dragon time to add or delete false documentation.

By tormenting the victim, the Dragon attempts to elicit an angry outburst, after which the victim quits in a public rage. At the very least, the Dragon can point out how unstable the victim is, thus supporting the contention that the employee deserved dismissal.

Dragon Tracks

- Have you ever been denied the joy of receiving appropriate compliments for a job that you know was done well?
- Are your assignments picked apart and criticized?
- Have deserved approval and promotion for a job well done been denied to you?
- Are you ignored, even when you have obviously done an excellent job?
- Are compliments and thank you notes that your boss receives about you ignored?
- Is such praise discarded so that it never appears on your permanent work record?
- Do undeserved letters of reprimand appear in your personnel file?
- Does your boss claim credit for your contributions?
- Did a Doorkeeper claim credit with your boss's approval?

Have You been Disciplined at Work Without a Legitimate Reason?

There are justifiable reasons for disciplinary action. They include:

1. Insubordination and other types of gross misbehavior
2. Drinking or taking drugs on the job
3. Larceny, stealing money or supplies from the company
4. Sabotage or deliberately doing inferior work

Discipline, however, does not have to mean punishment. Competent supervisors use an array of humane measures and try to reserve punishment only as a last resort. Punishment, by its very nature, is intended to hurt its recipient. There are varying degrees of punishment that differ in the amount of harm they inflict, from a simple word of reprimand to a physical beating. From the cruel crucifixion and torture chambers of the Middle Ages to the whip lashings administered in the name of *discipline* on sailing ships, despotic rulers have often used overly severe punishment to reinforce their power. Dragons, being despots, often gravitate toward this idea quickly and energetically. Dysfunctional work systems ruled by Dragons substitute punishment for discipline and use it for power, control, and intimidation.

Productive and honest employees are punished more often than others. Unfair disciplinary actions can mean time off without pay, a reduced salary, or denial of a well-deserved raise. A Dragon can find many ways to punish a targeted employee, either privately or publicly. Because it is almost always undeserved, Dragon-issued punishment will hurt a victim's sense of self-worth and make the job situation nearly intolerable. Punishment is closely linked with the power needs of an abuser. As one power-drunk Dragon summed it up, "Punishment lets people know who the boss is."

One Midwestern Dragon brought in a management trainer who bragged about how *punishment* can set the *base line foundation* for controlling employees. His primary points included:

- Punishment intimidates. Therefore, it takes away the targeted employee's power to resist. If the employee does resist, forbid it and degrade that person for doing so.
- Other staff members, fearing the same treatment, avoid the disciplined employee. This causes isolation of the targeted employee.
- Although discipline should be confidential, make sure to provide *information leaks* to intimidate other staff members.
- Punishment creates fear. Fearful employees are easily managed.

He concluded emphatically: "This is what it takes to get people to do a good job so that you can look good!"

Have You Been Given an Unrequested Transfer?

(See Chapter 3, Signature Pattern No. 5, Ostracizing.)

In an effort to create confusion, to make the job both painful and difficult, and to further isolate a person, Dragons will sometimes transfer victims from one Doorkeeper to another. The goal is to prove that the victim is inadequate in all job areas and consistently performs poorly, an accusation that the Doorkeepers are very willing to verify.

Playing "musical chairs" with the staff produces chaos, which is one of the Dragon's goals. If you are being transferred from one department to another, with a Doorkeeper boss in each of them, keep careful records in your DD.

Dragon Smoke

Irrational thoughts that the boss wants you to think:

I am feeling angry, and I do not know why. I must be going crazy. I hope the boss likes me even though I am criticized a lot. I feel nervous. I think I'll go get drunk. I will feel better tomorrow. It must be my home life; that's why I'm so upset. My spouse doesn't understand the stress that I am under. If it were not for my spouse, the bills, and the kids, I would not be stressed. I am afraid that if I am transferred again, I will lose my job. I can't say "no." A refusal would be the end of my employment here. My boss holds the key to everything that is worthwhile in my life. Without my job, I would be ruined. I had better do as I am told; the boss knows better than I what's good for me. I certainly do appreciate my boss. I am thankful that the company puts up with me. I am called names, but I probably deserve them. I will be the most cooperative worker this company has ever had.

(As one patient who had been in therapy for several years said, "It's easy to think that a bad job is better than no job..." until he learned how to Dragon-proof himself.)

Dragon-Taming Thoughts

Rational replacement thoughts:

These reprimands are completely unwarranted, and I have spotted abusive tactics aimed at me. Now my boss wants me to take a transfer, but I lack needed information about this transfer and the rationale behind it. I am not sure how much leeway I have, and I am determined to find out! I am going to make an appointment with my boss and respectfully decline the transfer. If my boss is a Dragon, I will not be successful. If my boss is a not a Dragon, I will have an opportunity to clarify my status within the company. Automatically accepting transfers that seem illogical makes no sense in terms of my career goals. I will document everything and take charge of my own future.

Dragon-Proofing Beliefs

I believe in myself. I believe in my ability to sense when things that are "fishy." I have the right to complete information about any transfer assigned to me. I believe that the boss has a right to transfer me without my permission but not without my knowledge. I have the right to free speech, and I intend to use it to speak up now. If I decide against the transfer, I have a right to say "no." I have courage. I will take the responsibility for my decisions, as well as my own future.

Comments

Since the boss wants you to get angry and put yourself at a disadvantage, you need to be aware of the alternatives to anger. To feel anger is perfectly normal for anyone who is abused. So, tune in to the anger energy and use it to research the pros and cons for the move. Then speak up about your concerns. If you decide that the transfer is not what you want, say "no" respectfully.

For example, you could say, "After thinking about the transfer, I have decided that I am probably not the best choice for the assignment. We both know that it is in the company's best interest to get a qualified person. Alicia and Joe both have more experience than I do for the position. Have you talked to X, Y, and Z? We could save a lot of company training time by transferring someone with their credentials if they would be willing to take on this assignment." Or perhaps, "I have been considering our discussion last week. I would like to take a pass on this transfer. It is not the kind of position at which I could really excel. I think I can come up with some alternatives, however, and I will get back to you tomorrow."

If your boss does not allow you to say "no," you have clear evidence that you are being forced out. It is time to take some definite steps toward making new career plans. Be sure to document everything and seek a legal opinion regarding your options. (See Chapter 12, Talk to a Lawyer.)

Is Your Job on the Line?

(See Chapter 3, Signature Pattern No. 2, Relationships and Chapter 4, Game No. 4, Musical Chairs.)

Virtually every abusive action directed toward a targeted employee who refuses to be a victim is aimed at a culminating meeting. The victim will be told, "Your job is on the line." This meeting often happens when the Dragon perceives the victim to be sufficiently confused, depleted, and unable to cope effectively with this new attack. It is very common for the victim to be told, "You are not proactive." It is difficult to defend against such a broad accusation. It is not easy to demonstrate whether a person is or is not "proactive," therefore it is a safe accusation for a Dragon to make. It will be implied that the victim has been under observation for quite some time and that performance has been poor. In some cases, victims have not received any previous warnings.

If the Dragon does not have enough ammunition to convince higher authorities to fire you, you will be given a new assignment and a specific time period within which you will be expected to prove yourself. You will be told that you must make changes, but you will not be given any specifics about what you did wrong in the first place and what changes are really expected. The Dragon might ramble on about having *heard complaints* and claim that many others have accused you of wrong doings, but you will not be told who was upset with you or why. In other words, you will not have the privilege of facing your accusers, if indeed there were any at all. In an effort to create a self-fulfilling prophecy, the Dragon will add that you are not expected to succeed.

You can turn this entire event around. As you leave the meeting, spot the Dragon ploys. Take an honest look at what is actually happening and face the fact that you are being attacked unfairly. You do not have to become obsessed with the job. You can trade your negative feelings for personal power once you recognize the power plays for what they are.

Sometimes victims do win. Here is an example of a time when an intended victim accidentally won the game of musical chairs:

> Pat wanted to work in the transportation department, but there were no openings. He accepted a position in Quality Control. Basically, his job was to red-flag errors in payroll reports, purchase orders, and billing. Almost immediately, he was approached with a deal. "All you have to do is look the other way, and we will make it worth your while. It's foolproof. We just deduct pennies - you know - rounded down from every account and assign them to this bogus account." Pat's reply was a firm, "No. And do not even bring up the subject to me again." Virtually overnight, he was called in for the "We have been watching you, and you're just not working out" speech followed by an immediate transfer across town to the transportation department (much to Pat's delight).

Was the deal-maker a Dragon or only a Doorkeeper? We will never know. What we do know is that he apparently had the power to create an immediate job opening where supposedly there was none.

Step IV Summary

Dragons, like abusers everywhere, use brainwashing to confuse or mystify their victims and then exert control over their lives. Dragons in the workplace psychologically torment victims by inducing fear while manipulating their basic belief systems in order to force compliance and subservience.

We have simplified the process of disarming Dragons by clearly labeling the sequence as:

Dragon Fire: What abusers do and say to victimize others

Dragon Smoke: What abusers want victims to believe in response to brainwashing

Dragon Taming: The rational replacement thoughts that resist mystification

Dragon Proofing: The expressions of personal power and freedom to choose that protect individuals from victimization

In Step IV, we demonstrated with a variety of examples exactly what workplace abusers do and what they expect their victims to think. Additionally, we have presented a variety of replacement thoughts, as well as examples of genuine beliefs, that can help victims to fight mystification and protect themselves from the effects of constant Dragon fire. To avoid becoming Dragon food, employees need to sort out their own realities from the brainwashing and thought control tactics that they experience from a Dragon.

We have intentionally presented our examples sequentially, from introductory "testing" to those that clearly send the signal that the victim is about to be forced out of the workplace. Becoming familiar with the typical power plays (from information control, pressuring, and subtle abuse to blatant harassment and building a contrived case for dismissal) gives intellectual control back to victims. Once these maneuvers are recognized as manipulative tactics carefully orchestrated to produce fear, they lose their power. A victim without fear regains personal power and is free to choose. A Dragon without *fear-inducing power* typically moves on to a new victim.

Discussion

Have you observed or experienced any of the activities described in Step IV?

Step V

Take Action

Now that you can spot Dragon behaviors and victimization strategies, it is important to realize that workers have more than the two options they typically gravitate toward: stay and be victimized or quit and be unemployed. Chapter 12, **Look at All the Options**, suggests coping with the workplace but only for a period of time while pursuing dozens of other options, suggestions, and ideas for disarming Dragons.

Chapter 13, **Do It**, urges readers to overcome procrastination and take definitive, positive steps toward dealing with their situations. To do so, they must review all their options, make choices, and then take responsible action. In the meantime, a number of helpful suggestions are provided:

- Planning ahead
- Testing your boss
- Keeping your sense of humor
- Staying in control
- Blocking abuse
- Knowing your rights
- Doing your homework
- Quitting
- Trying something new
- Scouting for Dragon tracks in a new workplace
- Staying in the old workplace while knowing that the boss is a Dragon
- Taming Dragons
- Making choices
- Dragon-proofing yourself
- Dealing with the Dragon's six signature patterns
- Getting on with your life

Chapter 12

Look at All the Options

Let's face it; everyone makes mistakes. We all get angry at one time or another. When the abuser attacks with put-downs, a fist slammed into a desk, or an object whizzing past your head, chances are you feel it in the pit of your stomach. Your hands shake as your body reacts to fury, terror, and threat. You control your impulse to retaliate, but it is as though your brain has deserted you, and you are struggling with two basic options: *stay* (and be abused) or *quit*! While it may feel like it, these are not the only two courses available. We have other ideas and suggestions, along with a number of *do's* and *don'ts*, for you to think about before you take decisive action.

The Third Option: "Timed Coping"

Consider a third option! You don't need to run away. You don't need to retaliate. You don't need to cringe with the boss's fury or turn into a Dragon yourself. Now that you know how Dragons operate, you don't need to be a victim. What you need is time–time to sort out options, get yourself together, and make your own plans without being shoved into an impossible predicament.

"Timed coping" is enduring abuse in the workplace for a set period of time, anywhere from a few days to a few months, while you carefully document what is happening before taking deliberate steps to exert more control over your future. By coping temporarily for a predetermined period, you will gain time to look at various options rather than being pressured into hasty decisions. By avoiding procrastination and retaining control of your life, you will learn about your own inner resources and feel your personal power grow. Getting in touch with your true values and basic beliefs gives you the courage to face any obstacles in your path.

Make a Timeline: Exercise 12-1

To help you decide how much time you are willing to spend on your current workplace dilemma, get in touch with your values, wants, and needs. Try a clarification exercise. You will need a pen, notebook, and a quiet place to work. After numbering a sheet of paper from 1 to 10, imagine this scenario:

You have been involved in a fatal automobile accident and have been told that you are now dead. It seems that you have just been denied entrance into the "executive suite," and you are sitting alone in the reception room. Apparently, there has been a computer problem, and you were not scheduled to pass through the Pearly Gates until tomorrow. You have a 24-hour reprieve.

Give yourself an appropriate amount of time (15 to 30 minutes) to list ten things that you really want to do before you go. When your list is complete, write down your answers to the following questions:

- Are there dreams, hopes, or goals on your list that need more than 24 hours to complete?
- If you could arrange for more time, perhaps six months, which items on your list could you possibly achieve?
- Are there some items that would take you a year or more to achieve?
- Where on your list is your career considered?
- Where do family concerns appear?

Make any changes to the list that you would like at this time. Keeping these ideas in mind, proceed to the next exercise.

Outline Some Tentative Goals for Yourself: Exercise 12-2

Date	*Tentative Goals* (Examples)
Ten years from today	Be in business for myself.
Five years from today	Finish college.
Next year	Change jobs.
Six months	Be prepared to make career decisions.
One month	"Time coping" ends – make decisions. Decide whether or not to relocate the family.
Two weeks	Gather information.
One week	Have a meeting with the boss to clarify issues.
Tomorrow	Talk to the family about my job and concerns.
Today	1. Check my Dragon diary – review my anecdotal records, job status, written evidence, and plans. 2. Make a list of phone numbers, i.e., attorney, EAP counselor, boss, personnel office.

Do It Now: Exercise 12-3

Think of one small step that you could take today toward achieving your most important goal.

Example: Discuss my work situation with loved ones.
Do a job search through the Internet.
Make an appointment with the boss.

Every plan has a beginning, and this is yours. It need not be complete. The point of these exercises is simply to jump-start your future planning.

Test the Boss: Exercise 12-4

Investigate Your Workplace: Is There Really A Dragon Here?

It is now time to test the supervisor to determine whether or not the person is actually a Dragon. Administer this test by scheduling a meeting with your supervisor and stating your case using direct eye contact:

- Tell the supervisor that you are concerned about the company and that you are interested in performing to the best of your ability.
- Calmly state that you intend to treat the supervisor with respect, and in return, you wish to be treated with the same respect due to any human being.
- Evaluate the supervisor.

For example, you might try an approach similar to this:

> Look Jacob, we are both interested in client satisfaction. Wouldn't you agree that we have worked together well (for the last year on the XYZ project)? I am sensing that something has changed, and I miss those days when

> we could have an honest talk. Part of the problem for me is the way we get along. I know that you are the boss, and I intend to continue treating you with the respect that you deserve. However, I too want to be treated with the respect due to any human being. Yelling at me, name-calling, or putting me down in front of others only makes things worse. I will do whatever it takes. If there is something that you want to get off your chest, I am all ears, but let's do it in private.

Perhaps another approach would work better in your situation:

> Wouldn't you agree that it would be better for the company if neither of us lost sight of the client? That seems to be a problem when we both get angry. I am suggesting that when we get upset, or if I am out of line, let's call a timeout. When we have both cooled off, we could take a coffee break together and have an honest, straightforward talk about the problem in private.

To determine whether or not your boss is a Dragon, request a specific appointment with your own specific question in mind. Evaluate what happens with your request according to the following list:

Test The Boss

A Dragon Boss Will:	*A Healthy Boss Will*:
Not set up an appoint with you	Set up an appointment as soon as possible
Send you to a Doorkeeper	**Listen carefully with good eye contact**
Block your access to hard information	Give hard information and attack the problems with you

A Dragon Boss Will:	*A Healthy Boss Will:*
Change the topic	**Stay focused on your topics and be interested in discussing the matter in detail**
Not listen to you	Be encouraged by your perceptiveness
Load you with responsibilities and busy work	**Perceive you as a team member interested in doing a good job**
Impose impossible standards, time schedules, and deadlines	Seriously consider your suggestions about adjusting working conditions
Generalize about your personality defects and not put anything in writing	**Be eager to clarify his or her decisions and put details in writing**
Predict you cannot live up to expectations while deliberately showing favoritism to colleagues	Give concrete examples of your strengths and weaknesses in the workplace
Threaten you with loss of position, status, or employment	**Detail job expectations for you**
Keep one-sided records of all negative encounters and use them to intimidate you	Have both positive and negative work records and use them them impartially

A Dragon Boss Will:	*A Healthy Boss Will:*
Never apologize for out-of-control behavior	**Apologize for any out-of-control moments**
Attack you with irrelevant "you" guns and "why" dagger questions	Refrain from any personal attacks and ask fair, sensible, relevant questions
Attack you personally instead of problems	**Appreciate your professionalism in alerting management to any potential trouble spots**
Label your efforts to clarify your situation as incompetence or dependency	Encourage your forthrightness in asking about improving the workplace
Avoid being alone with you, preferring public ridicule or punishment	**Give you direction and guidance relative to your concerns; complimenting in public while confronting in private**

If you receive specific and reasonable answers, your boss is probably not a Dragon. In this case, positive changes may result from leveling with the boss. If your boss is a Dragon, however, expect an attempt to bully you and do not expect positive changes.

Act as Though: Exercise 12-5

Give Yourself an Opportunity to Experience Your Workplace in a Positive Manner

Have you tried quitting your job in your mind? Imagine that you have found a new position just across the street from the one in which you are presently employed. The job description is the same;

the pay and work sites are identical. The difference is that the new position is in a functional organization, and your boss is not a Dragon. There are no Doorkeepers or Doormats with whom to contend.

With this new scenario in mind, ask yourself these questions:

- How would you feel about going to work tomorrow?
- How would you dress on the first day at the new job?
- How would you feel as you opened the door?
- How would you act?
- With whom would you speak?
- How would you spend your time during breaks?
- What attitude would you bring with you to the new job?
- What new ideas or inspirations might you feel ready to tackle?
- What special talents and skills do you have to offer at the new workplace?
- How would you go about becoming involved with the new staff?
- What would be the psychological difference between this workplace and the old one?
- How would your attitude change?

Now take this new attitude for one day and go back to your current workplace, putting in everything that you have imagined during this exercise. Disregard whatever you normally expect from others and *act as though* you were really beginning a new job. *Act as though* you were happy, excited about the work, eager to impress the boss, ready to make new friends on the job, and willing to contribute generously with your energy and talent. You may find, as many others have, that things begin to change. Try this powerful experiment for a week before making a decision about leaving your current position.

Tim's Story

Tim, an industrial engineer for a medium-sized company, felt stressed and angry about the abusive treatment that he and others were receiving from their supervisor. Originally, he thought that it was the job itself that was bothering him, but enough conversations with his supervisor finally convinced him that the core problem was one of supervision. He went through a series of thoughts somewhat like these:

- It is not the job that is bugging me.
- It is the boss who is being destructive; he has changed.
- I'm not willing to be abused.
- I really love this type of work.
- I'm not the only one being abused in this office.
- I need to talk to somebody about this situation.

He went to the company EAP counselor who recognized symptoms of workplace abuse. She advised Tim to try the *act as though* system - psychologically quitting his job as described above and *acting as though* he loved it.

After one week of experiencing Tim's positive attitude and behaviors, coworkers began noticing some relief in their own stress levels and went to the same counselor for help. With the sudden influx of clients, the counselor recognized the signature patterns of an abusive boss and went to work. The office workers received counseling.

The boss, who had gradually turned Dragon-like, was referred for chemical dependency treatment. Tim transferred to another department within the company but soon returned when the boss completed treatment successfully. The company retained two valuable employees and remained financially healthy and viable. There was much less stress in that particular workplace, and the boss's behavior was much improved.

Keep Your Sense of Humor

Learn to laugh at yourself; cultivate your funny bone. It is biochemically impossible to be depressed and have a good laugh at the same time. Increasingly, research evidence indicates that laughter is good medicine for both mind and body.

The staff at a Midwestern office was able to cope with their Dragon until his early departure by refusing to take his outrageous ravings seriously. They quietly circulated the following anecdote:

Two staff members were overhead discussing their summer-break activities:

Sue: ". . . and from Switzerland, I visited Paris."

Lou: "Fantastic."

Sue: "After visiting Monaco, I had tea with the Queen of England."

Lou: "Fantastic!"

Sue: "And what did you do this summer?"

Lou: "Oh, nothing so exciting! I just took a course in Split-Second Diplomacy 101 at the university."

Sue: "Really, how interesting! Tell me, what did they teach you?"

Lou: "It's called the F-system. Whenever you feel like saying the "F-word," just substitute the word "Fantastic!"

While granting their boss the superficial respect that his title warranted, the staff found many occasions to keep their humor alive. They managed to extinguish the force of their boss's Dragon fire with exclamations of "How Fantastic!"

Visualize Your Boss in a Humorous Situation

When resisting verbal abuse by controlling your emotions, it helps to see your abuser in a position of your own creation. For example, instead of concentrating on Dragons behind huge desks, imagine them as infants sitting in highchairs, dressed only in diapers with cereal dripping out of their mouths, babbling and screaming. Your one problem may be to keep yourself from laughing as you do so. Other visualizations that have been used successfully include: seeing your abuser as an animal (a pig wallowing in the mud, a baboon shouting from its cage, or an ant about to be squashed by a giant foot) or a paper-mache Dragon with a miniature human inside desperately trying to eject fire from its mouth to create a ferocious appearance.

Stay in Control

Don't Backbite

Like a dysfunctional family system, a dysfunctional workplace is almost always in some level of denial. No matter how unfairly treated you feel, seeking revenge by badmouthing the boss is never a good move. Discussing your personal anger issues with colleagues, conducting your own opinion polls, or gathering support for your cause among other employees does nothing for you. These attempts to rally support only perpetuate the misery of other employees.

Sidestep the Personal Attack

Try to sidestep the boss's attack by ignoring the personal and changing the topic back to the problem. Acknowledge the Dragon's position and then change the topic to a neutral one or a business concern. For example:

Boss: You %&# idiot. What the hell is wrong with you? I don't care about your idiotic ideas. No one told you to change anything. Now keep your mouth shut and do as you are told around here or you'll be on unemployment next month with the rest of the deadheads.

You: I hear you. What is it about the changes that you see as unworkable? How do you want the ABC situation handled?

Block Verbal Abuse Nonverbally

If nothing you do seems to stop the verbal abuse that you must endure in order to keep your job, try a nonverbal deterrent. Keep a small tape recorder visible. You do not have to use it, but it will serve as a nonverbal reminder to your abusers that you have the equipment to record their assaults verbatim.

Do Call a Timeout

You cannot reason with an enraged person, whether it is a Dragon or not. Both parties will need time and space to calm down before you can deal with your anger and think clearly. Take the initiative, but do it with dignity. Speak of the overt intent in the Dragon's message while supporting the boss's position and setting up a later engagement to clarify issues. For instance:

Boss: You lamebrain! You never get things done on time! You'll never make it at this job. If you don't shape up, I'm not going to renew your contract. Your attitude isn't what I expect from my employees.

You: I realize that you are concerned. I would like to discuss the timelines in more detail after I have calmed down and given your words some serious thought. How about tomorrow afternoon? Would 4:00 fit your schedule?

The nasty message is probably only Dragon smoke, and most likely, the boss doesn't really want to discuss timelines with you. In such a case, it's unlikely that you will get an appointment, but you'll probably get more Dragon fire. Don't take it personally. Simply put physical space between you and the Dragon. If your boss is not a Dragon, however, your plan to give his words serious thought after you both have calmed down is a good move.

Do Block Abuse When It Occurs

Develop a thick skin and a tin ear. Realize that the Dragon has the anger problem. Refuse to respond to provocations, no matter how intense they become. Remember that in order to be a Doormat, you must first lie down. Stick to the issues, and do not sacrifice your dignity. For example:

Boss: You idiot! Can't you follow a simple directive? How in the #@% can I get things done when I have to come out here and read simple English to pinheads like you!

You: Yes, boss. Exactly which directive are you concerned about, the one you gave me yesterday or the new version that you just sent me? I'm human; I could have misinterpreted your intent. I will be happy to follow the one that you think is best, but as I see it, there is no need for name-calling.

Cut 'Em off at the Pass

You may have already determined not to invest any more time in a dysfunctional system. You might be ready to leave. If you are unable to stop the abuse through a private talk, then it is up to you to take control of the situation. You may be fired for insubordination, but it may work to give you a little more time to mend fences before you go.

Be as respectful and calm as you can but walk away as you say:

You: Yes, Boss. Can you meet me in the office? I consider these personal attacks abusive. I am unwilling to be abused. Therefore, I am leaving until we both calm down. I have

> time to meet with you at 9:00 a.m., but I can meet at another time if it is more convenient for you.

Remember, if you act like a victim, you are one.

Make Sure You See the Dragon's "You" Gun

In Chapter 9, we described the "you" gun. Both Dragons and Doorkeepers are "you" gun marksmen. When the abuser shoots you down with a volley of "you's" followed by derogatory and abusive remarks, learn to see the invisible pointing finger. The index finger points to you, the victim, but the three other fingers are pointing back at the abuser.

Psychologically, the abusers are projecting on to you the denied insecurities about themselves that are part of the Dragon/Doormat pathology. To realize that abusers are actually revealing secrets about themselves (which they may not even be aware of) helps you to survive in an atmosphere of blame and shame. The Dragons call you an idiot because they secretly harbor insecurities about their own ability level and fear you will find out. So keep your self-respect by keeping the Dragon's secret insecurity confidential but use your insight to weather the cheap shots.

Put It in Writing

Document! Document! Document! But Keep Unbiased Records

Continue to document everything that has been happening to you. If you have not started to do this, it's time to begin. Keep all of your records at home. Do not enter anything into the computer at work that must remain private. Resist the temptation to make the records sound biased in your favor. Factual and neutral wording is best.

> Bob, a senior supervisor in a statewide transportation system, recognized that a supervisor, who had more status and power than Bob, was abusive. This

person had demanded that Bob and his assistant, Kenny, keep detailed but biased records on the activity of a certain designated employee in order to build a case for legal dismissal.

Bob complied with his order to keep records but refused to be intimidated into being unfair. He kept complete records on all employees that included both negative and positive incidents. He also recorded all contacts with the Dragon, including his demands, threats, and intimidation verbatim.

Bob refused to dismiss the targeted employee because the records being kept by Kenny, which were requested by the boss, were negatively biased and incomplete. During Bob's vacation, Kenny and the boss dismissed the victim for alleged tardiness and excessive absences.

When the employee filed a legal complaint on the grounds of discrimination, just a glance at Bob's unbiased records, submitted to the legal staff, showed quite clearly that the charges by the Dragon were unfair. The dated and detailed records identified without doubt the Dragon-like part played by the boss, the intimidation of the Doorkeeper assistant, and the dysfunctional climate in the workplace.

The case never went to court; the evidence was clearly in favor of the plaintiff. The organization quickly made changes in its supervisory staff, and the victim was rehired with back pay, apologies, and an eventual promotion.

Do Your Homework

Discrimination and sexual abuse are illegal. Most organizations have specific written policies for dealing with abuse issues. Learn about personnel resources in your company. Research grievance procedures and let the personnel director know that you have requested respectful treatment and that you are documenting your concerns. Collect information on transfer policies and request letters of recommendation from those who know your professionalism and your work performance.

Know Your Rights

Check Out Your Employment Contract

If you are working under contract, you and your employer probably have agreed that you will not quit and that they will not discharge you as long as certain conditions exist. Usually, there is a policy wherein management retains the right to evaluate, make suggestions, and issue warnings and probation periods before termination occurs. In general, if the contract calls for a two-month notice before termination, the employee must give a two-month notice before quitting, unless both parties agree to change the contract.

Traditionally, working without a contract meant that you were employed "at will" or that the boss had the right to hire or fire you without notice or reason. Unless you were a slave, workers also had the right to quit. In many countries throughout the world, these conditions still exist. In the free world, however, there are many protections. In the United States, union contracts and legislative acts require nondiscriminatory employment and management procedures.

Employment without a contract is usually considered "at will," but this is not always the case. Take a look at the company's policy manuals, guidelines, employment applications, license applications, and other written documents. Unless they clearly state that the organization is an "at-will" employer, you may be working under a contract-of-sorts that gives you more rights than you think. Even without a contract, employers may not break federal laws. Since state and provincial laws and court decisions vary, it is always best to seek legal consultation if you are concerned about your rights.

Contract or no contract, employees cannot be forced to waive their right to sue for discrimination.

Consult a Professional About Your Legal Options

Talk To An Attorney

Do not wait until things are extremely serious before contacting someone about your legal options. The corporate lawyer already has a client - your boss - so skip that option! The attorney-client confidentiality is guaranteed, so you will want to look for someone with whom you can speak openly and someone whom you respect. Look for a person you can trust who has an ethical track record and some expertise in your problem. You may want to begin your search with attorneys who specialize in labor law or personal injury.

An effective lawyer knows and upholds the law, protects your rights, communicates well, and doesn't use a cannon when a peashooter will do. A good attorney will inform you of your rights but will let you know when you are wrong. The person you choose should be more interested in directing you to arbitration or mediation services than in retaliation.

When you hire an attorney, you are renting expertise and professional skill to resolve your problem. Legal help may range from a few hours of counsultation about what you can do for yourself to formal letters from your lawyer expressing your concerns. Such letters should be succinct and stated in such a way that your rights are heard and taken seriously. If everything else fails, a suit may be necessary.

We believe that the costs of legal counsel are a bargain for anyone dealing with a Dragon, especially when compared to the price for not consulting one in terms of unwarranted stress and emotional scars that can last for years. Ethical lawyers always clarify fees and answer your questions regarding financial matters early in the process. Let's look at what might be involved legally should you decide that your boss is a Dragon and that you are being victimized.

Such disputes are usually civil cases as opposed to criminal ones. Basically, a civil case begins with a complaint by one party (the plaintiff) and a response from the other (the defendant). In the process of defining the issue, there may be several levels of communication before one side files the formal complaint. After the complaint is filed and served, the defendant will reply with an answer denying all or part of the allegations of the complaint.

At that point the issue has been *joined,* and pretrial preparations begin. This procedure can consist of "discovery," in which the parties serve written questions to one another in an attempt to gain more information about the claim. Each side will potentially use the answers in their own defense. Later, if necessary, depositions of the various parties and witnesses are taken. These depositions consist of questioning under oath to determine the extent of the person's knowledge about the case.

Most cases do not actually go to trial and are settled by mutual agreement. In some cases, just the sight of a well-respected attorney having lunch with the victim in the corporate dining room can be enough to stimulate a positive change in formerly abusive working conditions. Cases can be settled by mutual agreement before filing, before trial, during jury deliberation, and even after a verdict. No matter how the dispute is resolved, even if you mediate the issue yourself, it is best to get the advice of your lawyer and have it put in writing before signing anything.

What About Quitting?

Don't Be A Martyr

The dysfunctional system supports the Dragon/Doorkeepers symbiosis. You can do little to change the system while still a part of it. Whistle-blowers have a long history of being blackballed, discriminated against, and destroyed. It boils down to "*kill the messenger*" in a dysfunctional system. Once you have survived the career change, you are in a much more solid position to speak up, and your voice can be heard.

Don't Just Quit

No matter how good it might feel to say, "You can't fire me, I quit," consider the consequences. By quitting, you lose unemployment insurance and often other benefits to which you may be entitled. Some people believe that quitting looks better on a resume then being fired. In reality, employers no longer use the words, *fired* or *quit* on written references, and they are good words to purge from your vocabulary when you think about a resume or application for future employment. Business jargon includes more current synonyms such as:

Left by Mutual Agreement:

We made a deal; we have agreed on the date that you are leaving and the date that the company will stop paying your salary.

Terminated:

Legally, it is a business decision. It usually means that some rules were broken and could cover practically anything from insubordination to theft or assault. The company does not want to make specific charges in black and white.

Staff Cutback:

There is work but none for you. The company simply sidesteps the reasons why they do not need (or want) you. Dysfunctional workplaces love to use this one in playing musical chairs with employees. (See Chapter 4, Power Game No. 4.)

Reorganization:

We cannot find any legal reason to fire you. In a dysfunctional system, it means that you have not become a willing victim, you will not quit, and you are a threat to the Dragon-in-residence.

(Maybe you've been seen reading this book.) We have to be careful about exactly how we pick on you. You may be demoted or relocated. When the heat is off, you will be downsized out of the company (if the Dragon still has power).

Downsizing:

We are eliminating job categories with no hope of rehiring in order to reduce company costs. The job categories with the most seniority and the largest payrolls will be the first to go. Note: Longitudinal research indicates that in the years following downsizing, the original number of employees is regained or exceeded, but the new employees are inexperienced and vulnerable. Often, it is a smoke-and-mirrors strategy to make the payroll budget look good while other expenses skyrocket.

Layoff could mean:

We have eliminated our vulnerable employees because of adverse business conditions.

Laid-off workers usually are eligible for unemployment compensation for a designated period of time. People who are still around when the organization resumes hiring have a chance of going back to work.

Personality Conflict:

In workplace jargon these words imply that it is the employee's personality that is in conflict with someone else's. It is up to these employees to learn how to grovel and say, "Yes sir," appropriately to management. Nowhere is there any hint that management could be infiltrated with Dragons and Doorkeepers who generate the conflict then blame their victims.

There are many excellent self-help references that address topics relevant to getting along with difficult people. However, if the abuser is a Dragon, no amount of *blame the victim - shape up the victim - teach them to tolerate more abuse* tactics will change the dysfunctional workplace into a functional one.

Put Worries Aside

Don't Worry About Negative References

Most employers adhere to the policy of never passing on negative evaluations to another party. They know that the voice on the other end of the phone could be your lawyer. Some also know the term "constructive discharge" and hope that you do not.

You see, some employers worry that if they fire a person, the person who is no longer under their control will give them grief. So, they deliberately set out to make the employee so miserable that the person will leave peacefully on his or her own. They step up their abuse tactics for a period of time. They might give the victim unpleasant assignments, overly monitor all activities including restroom breaks, create reasons to use blame or shame for minor infractions, and deliberately put pressure on until the employee breaks down emotionally or physically and quits or retires early. The courts, however, have decreed that when any employee quits as a result of intentionally unfair treatment on the job, the departure is termed "constructive discharge." The plaintiff is entitled to all back pay, as well as rehiring or a satisfactory financial settlement.

Your current employer might be reluctant to release negative information about you to any future employers and might prefer to give only basic information, such as your job title and dates of employment. Furthermore, if your recommendation is too positive, your future employer may suspect that you are a troublemaker and that your present organization is hoping to get rid of you. We have heard of employees who have had a friend phone former employers asking for verification of references to find out exactly what is being said about them.

Try Something New

Interview for a New Position

Interview for a new position just for the experience and practice, especially for a job that you are interested in but not sold on. Now that you know how to explain your motivation for a career move, the next step is to know what is fair and what is not in an employment interview.

It is illegal to discriminate against anyone on the basis of age, race, ethnicity, sex, religion, physical or mental disabilities, or national origin. Some interviewers will ask open-ended questions permitting you to bring up such topics if you wish, but actually pinning you down in any of these areas is illegal.

For example, you can be asked about any "convictions" for felonies but not about your arrest record. The reasoning is that you are innocent until proven guilty in the United States. Judging anything by an arrest record alone is discriminatory. So be prepared for broadly based questions such as, "Are you over 17 years of age?" or "State your date of birth and the year you graduated from school," and not "How old are you?"

Did you know that it is illegal for an employer to refuse to hire an applicant over the age of 40 just because of age? Did you know that it is illegal to pressure older employees to retire by repeatedly asking them to do so? The term *overqualified* to reject an older candidate is also no longer a safe ploy for employers.

If the employer breaks all rules and asks improper questions such as, "Are you planning on having more children?" It may be a red flag that you are applying for a position in a questionable organization. Be cautious and watchful of the situation. You may want to gain some more information about the company before committing either way.

The penalty for an organization that violates the law generally involves making amends by hiring the applicant with back pay beginning from the date of the interview or reaching reasonable financial settlement. But why work for a company like this? Why tolerate the hassle of proving discrimination in court? It is better to use the interview as a learning tool and get on with your life.

If the interview goes well, you may consider employment with the company. You have enhanced your own personal power, self-esteem, and list of options – a win-win deal for you!

Using Your New Skills, Conduct a Preliminary Dragon Inspection

Don't Switch to Another Dysfunctional Organization

If you are considering taking a new position, visit the site. You can tell a lot about the working climate by the nonverbal and verbal communication that you pick up. Do employees laugh, smile, and speak cordially to one another? Are they relaxed or are they rigid, tight-lipped, and stiffly courteous to each other? Do things change when a person in authority is present? You might even check things out with an employee or two by asking such things as the following questions. "Do you like your job here?" "What makes this organization a good place to work?" "Are there any drawbacks to working here?"

Pay attention to *how* the answer is given as well as to *what* is actually said. Remember that abuse in the workplace has a domino effect. Does the person you are speaking to glance around before answering? Any hedging or qualifying can be a warning that you need to look a little closer to be sure that this organization is worthy of your application.

Cyndi's Story

Cyndi, a recent high school graduate, entered Restaurant A and asked to see the manager about her scheduled employment interview.

Employee: Why? You don't want to work here do you? If you're smart, you'll get out of here now, while you can.

Cyndi: Oh, you're just kidding, aren't you? Things can't be that bad. Are they?

Employee: You'll find out.

The interview went well. She was hired on the spot. The manager immediately rearranged the other employees' schedules to accommodate Cyndi's availability. Cyndi noticed that the employees appeared to be tense, quiet, and poorly groomed. At one point, the manager joked, "It's OK [that] you don't smoke. It won't be long before you'll be smoking and drinking just like the rest of us." He pointed out that all personal effects were to be locked away during working hours and that Cyndi was to report to him if she experienced any type of harassment. She left with her new uniform and employment papers in hand, scheduled to begin work the following day.

Though excited about her new job, she felt uneasy about her experience and the apparent tension in the workplace. Instead of canceling her next employment interview for a nearby restaurant, she did her own research.

Cyndi checked out Restaurant B as a customer, just before closing time and prior to her employment interview. She noted workers busily engaged in their respective tasks. They seemed relaxed, courteous, and friendly. When the doors closed for the evening, music came from the kitchen. Soon several employees joined in singing. Others chatted and joked as they worked.

Cyndi asked to see the manager regarding her employment interview.

Employee: He'll be right with you. Are you're applying to work with us? We can use another person.

Cyndi: Great! I like the music you're playing in the kitchen.

Employee: Yeah, you'll love it here. I hope you get the job!

Her interview went well and Cyndi was offered employment. The manager explained that to be fair, he needed a week to consult with existing staff and adjust schedules to accommodate a new person. Cyndi noticed employee lockers without locks and was told that padlocks were available should anyone care to use them.

Cyndi returned her uniform to Restaurant A and waited a week for employment at Restaurant B. She never regretted trusting her feelings and doing research before accepting employment.

Be Your Own Boss

Consider Self-Employment

Advancements in technology have ushered in many opportunities for nontraditional employment and entrepreneurships. Close supervision is no longer necessary in many decentralized industries and sales organizations. Teams of people located at distances both large and small from the parent organization are replacing the traditional systems. Telecommuters need only to meet periodically with their self-directed teams, which may make the old line-and-staff paradigm of power and control obsolete in the future.

As business goals change, priorities change. Many organizations are using subcontractors for operations that formerly would have been considered essential. A large corporation, for instance, might contract with groups of computer programmers from India or China in order to meet a deadline. Another company may subcontract their payroll to an independent firm specializing exclusively in time-keeping, check writing, and direct-deposit payroll payment operations. Many smaller businesses contract out packing, shipping, billing, bookkeeping, and marketing.

With just a little imagination, you can think of a number of possibilities for becoming your own boss. Think about becoming an independent contractor; find a need and fill it. What are your skills or your special talents? What part of your job could be done at home? How could the organization become more efficient by dropping its side operations and focusing its efforts more clearly on its major functions?

Be Your Own Boss Brainstorming: Exercise 12-6

The point of this exercise is to free-associate; you should allow your ideas to flow spontaneously without evaluating them as good, bad, possible, or impossible. Add as many items to your lists as you can and do not worry about duplications or practicality. Just start this list, put it aside, and then come back to it again whenever you have another idea. Solicit suggestions from others.

1. Think about your workplace, identify your company's major goal, and then add subordinate goals.
2. What are the little distractions that tax your time?
3. What parts of your operation are expendable?
4. What are your talents?
5. What are your interests?
6. What skills do you have?
7. What skills would you like to develop?
8. Do you have any additional thoughts that don't fit within any of the above categories?

Put your brainstorming exercise aside for a few days and then add some more ideas. When ready, check the lists for ideas that might inspire you or at least tickle your imagination. Pull out those ideas and do some fantasy planning as follows:

My Best Ideas Are:

Because:

Update Your Knowledge and Skills

Consider Going Back To School

Going back to school makes sense if you have a specific goal in mind. Check the job market first. Current information is as close as your own computer, the public library, school counselor's office, or university placement service, and it's free for the asking. If you're really interested in a new program, or to check if you truly need it, examine the local market for graduates by applying for the position you believe you will be seeking when you have completed the program. This experience will give you a better sense of what these employers are looking for and whether you meet their requirements. Unless the new career requires a license or certification, you may find that you already qualify for employment without further course work.

Retire to Another Career

Launch Your Dreams

Today, the smart employee always has two or more career tracks in mind: one major, one minor, and another just for enjoyment - a hobby, a special interest or a retirement dream. Taking advantage of a company retirement plan to launch your next career move is a good idea for many people. Research tells us that those who retire into careers stay productive, alert, active, and actually live longer than those who do not. Perhaps you are not a Grandma Moses or a Colonel Sanders, but you can be a Carl Musgrave. A gifted artist, Carl used his early retirement funds to launch his dream: a studio, an art gallery, and a teaching career.

Don't Burn Bridges – Leave with a Smile

Make a Positive Exit

If your boss is a Dragon, your company is or soon will be dysfunctional. Perhaps the system is still in denial, perhaps not. Eventually, the dysfunction will be felt, the Dragon/Doorkeeper pattern will end, and the business will most likely fail. In the meantime, get on with your life and your career rather than joining the dysfunctional system. If the system regains health and workers can again pay attention to business rather than jump psychological hurdles just to remain productive, you may wish to return. Gather letters of recommendation for your file long before letting it be known publicly that you are considering leaving. Keep copies of your letters at home in your private file.

Write a Positive Resignation Letter

If you decide to move on with your career, do not allow negative emotions to permeate any written correspondence between you and your employer. The cardinal rule has always been that if you want to be successful in the business world, be gracious as you come or go. The doors in business swing both ways. Never say anything uncomplimentary about your present or past employers in public. The universal white lie is that a person always leaves a position because of *"an offer I just couldn't refuse."* You may wish to return some day as an independent consultant. Nasty resignation letters have a way of following you despite so-called rules of confidentiality.

In your letter, you should:

- Find reasons to support the company or the business effort.
- Point out, with names if you wish, those individuals who made life on the job bearable and thank them for their assistance, support, professionalism, etc. Note: Sometimes the use of names of supporters could set those people up for future targeting by the Dragon boss.
- Be as honest and forthright as possible about the things you learned and/or the positive memories that you are taking with you.
- Keep your dignity intact.

Here is a sample of an informal resignation letter:

Dear ___________:

Please accept my resignation from ABC Company as of July 31. I wish to thank all of you for your support and encouragement throughout the years, especially Sally who spent so many hours deciphering my handwriting and editing my copies. As I move ahead in my career, I leave with mixed memories. The ones I value the most are those when we overcame all obstacles and won the Clark contract. Such professionalism is hard to find.

I will be watching the company's progress and cheering you all on in spirit. Please forward my mail to: (home address).

If a positive letter from you would be totally dishonest emotionally, then stick to the truth, be businesslike, formal, and dignified. Avoid stooping to retaliation, character assassination, or accusations. Remember, if the company challenges any of your accusations, you will have the burden of proof.

A verbal resignation is all that is actually necessary, but it is best to have a written record that dates your departure formally, especially if there may be litigation in the future. Keep these tips in mind:

- Be brief
- Be cordial
- Be clear
- Don't explain why you are leaving
- Be formal
- Send a letter:

  Dear Dr. Villani:

  Please accept my resignation from the University of Lakeville as Senior Psychologist effective October 31.

  Respectfully,
  Dough Re Me, Ph.D.

- Send a memo

  M E M O

  Date: September 1, 2003

  From: John Q. Doe, Media Specialist

  To: Harriet Osborn, Personnel Director

  Re: Resignation

  This is to tender my resignation from Murphy and Gillim Associates as of October 31, 2003.

Chapter 13

Do It!

Are you a *procrastinator*? It has been said that a journey of a thousand miles always begins with one step. Often that first step is a barrier, but once it is overcome, the others quickly follow. Putting decisions off, feeling stuck, or waiting to see what happens before making a move can be old habits acquired from previous impulsive or negative experiences.

Breaking Free

Is it *fear* that underlies your hesitation or is it *caution?* Caution based upon experience can usher in direction, security, and decisiveness; whereas fear is often irrational and can be immobilizing. The first move toward overcoming procrastination is attacking fears, especially those most common to people who have been working in a dysfunctional setting. The following exercises will give you some ideas for confronting those fears. You may want to use several pages of your Dragon diary for these exercises.

So What: Exercise 13-1

Part 1

1. Make a list, beginning with your worst fear. This is the hardest part. Some of us would rather visit the dentist for a root canal than admit that we are afraid. Putting your biggest fear in writing is like turning on the lights for a child who fears the dark. It makes the fear manageable.
2. Think about the worst thing that could happen if you dealt with the fear and write that down.
3. Think about the best thing that could happen if you dealt with that fear and write that down.
4. Now speculate about what might be the most likely outcome should you take action toward dealing with that fear.

Part II

Now go back to the negative answers that you wrote and dispute them. Be the Devil's advocate. Think, "So what!" Put your disputed thoughts in parentheses. Use humor and creativity to deal with those fears. Add encouraging comments whenever you can. Example:

1. *My worst fear is* – talking to my boss. (He never listens anyway; **so what's** the big deal!)
2. *Worst thing that could happen is* – I would throw up. (**So what!** I could throw up on the boss – sounds like a great idea!)
3. *Best thing that could happen is* – I would get a transfer. (**So what!** A transfer is better than being Dragon food.)
4. *Most likely* – I would tell him that I want a transfer, but I wouldn't get it, and I would feel foolish. (**So what!** It wouldn't be the first time I felt foolish. I guess I could handle that, especially if I got a transfer.)

---

1. *My next fear is* – If I don't get a transfer, I will have to find another job. (**So what**! I was looking for a job when I got this one!)
2. *The worst thing that could happen is* – I would not find another job. (**So what!** I'll ask my brother-in-law for help. He owes me!)
3. *The best thing that could happen is* – I could find a better position. (Yes! That's a great move – I'll see what can be done!)
4. *The most likely thing that could happen is* – I would have to stay where I am while I search for another position. (**So what!** I've done that before. I don't especially like the process, but I can handle it.)

Use your Dragon diary to explore your fears in writing. For example:

Hypothetical		*So What!*
My fear is:	Talking to the boss.	(If he yells, I'll be expecting it.)
The worst outcome is:	I might throw up.	(If I feel nauseated, I'll aim for the boss!)
The best outcome:	I will get a transfer.	(If I don't ask, I'll never be considered for the move.)
The probable outcome:	I'll ask, and he'll say "no!"	(So what's the big deal; "no" is his favorite word. I don't have to accept it. I can continue with my own plans to leave.)

Choice Is Your Responsibility – And So Are the Results

If your boss is a Dragon, you can choose to stay or you can choose to leave. You have a free will; you can survive the temporary distress of making changes. You can also cope with Dragons and Doorkeepers, now that they are unmasked and you have many new skills to aid you in the effort. If you elect to stay in your position despite knowing that you are working with a Dragon, expect to become an expert in anger control, stress management, and Dragon-proofing.

Taking responsibility for your choices isn't always as easy as it seems. Any major shift in lifestyle brings unfamiliar stresses and old habits into play. A battered spouse chooses to leave, yet often returns. If your boss is a Dragon, it may take you a short time to adjust to your new vantage point and experience the freedom that comes from having choices again.

What Is Your Job Worth to You?

So *Your Boss Is a Dragon, and You're Considering Staying...*

Now that medical researchers have made genuine breakthroughs in understanding and documenting how the mind-body connection works, there is little doubt about the role prolonged negative stress has on physical illness and longevity. We know that attitude can make a big difference in what works for you and what works against you. Optimism, curiosity, a sense of well-being, emotional strength, and the desire to attack new tasks each day can enhance your physical health. On the other hand, intense and prolonged negative stress, anger, isolation, confusion, depression, and entrapment (all part of your experience with Dragons) have quite the opposite effect.

Those at high risk for long-term emotional consequences from the negative stress are often those who have had previous experiences with victimization: witnessing abusive spousal relationships, rigid or abusive parenting, and authoritarian or military schooling. These people can be in denial and may even be attracted to the familiar "victim role" in the workplace. Typically, they present no outward indications of distress, but they can erupt into violence quite unexpectedly when subjected to prolonged abuse in a dysfunctional workplace.

Another group at high risk may have never had any abusive experiences – they are the "pleasers." They are often naive and do anything to please or gain the acceptance of others. They are the optimists who try to deal with their difficulties either by changing themselves or attempting to think like a Dragon. Their futile hope is that their efforts will in some way affect the boss's behavior.

However, Dragons, by definition, simply don't change; those who remain captivated by their power do.

Those at low risk for negative consequences are high-energy people who see every day as a challenge. They make their work central to their lives and give as much time to the process of transforming negative stress into positive energy in the workplace as the athlete does to train for the Olympics. The pitfalls, of course, can be numerous when one deliberately chooses to put all emotions aside in favor of a logical move or when one selfishly denies the social impact of a decision made through blind logic rather than balanced reasoning. The secret to success, it seems, is the old concept of the golden mean, finding a balance among emotions and logic, living each day to the fullest, and possessing a willingness to take limited risks.

Prepare Yourself for Stress

In their book, *The Longevity Strategy*, Dr. Richard Restak and David Mahoney quote clinical psychologist Wayne Sotilel as saying, "Your chances of living a long and healthy life depend on how successfully you manage stress in your daily life. Perhaps no other area of brain-body interaction is as important as this, and perhaps no other is so much within your ability to influence." Restak and Mahoney propose that humans are capable of living to be 100 years old using the brain-body connection and balancing not only the workplace but also relationships, the family, and the self as well. This idea is based on the belief that concentrating on only one area - usually work - causes stress.

In his book, *Stress for Success*, sports psychologist James Loehr suggests a balanced training program for developing one's ability to handle stress and to focus and transform it into positive energy in the workplace. Both of these books are excellent resources if you intend to remain working with a Dragon.

Freedom Is the Key to Making a Healthy Choice

By making the free choice to remain working within an abusive workplace, you are taking charge of your future. Make sure you are not trapped into the decision and you have a clear understanding of your alternatives. Prepare yourself with the opportunity to change your decision. So, if (1) yours is a free choice from among many options, (2) you're looking forward to the experience of dealing with your Dragon, and (3) you don't have family obligations to consider, then go for it!

- You know how victimization works.
- You can track the Dragon and Doorkeepers by their signature patterns.
- You can be prepared for the subtle, as well as the obvious, power plays.
- You can resist brainwashing.
- You can disarm the Dragon and Dragon-proof yourself.
- You may be able to uncover the secrets underlying the dysfunction in the workplace.

Be Sure You Have an Exit Available

Adding the stress of dealing with a Dragon to the typical job stress at work can be masochism at its worst, and ordinarily, we would not suggest this alternative. However, if you love risk taking and you're the type who enjoys quick moves, you may be one of the few who can manage to work with a Dragon.

Prepare Yourself

- Review the five steps presented in this book. Learn all you can about how the Dragon operates in your setting.
- Spot the Dragon tracks. By staying alert and aware, you will avoid the confusion most victims report.
- Stay in touch with your feelings.
- If anger signals a problem, deal with it.
    1. Abuse me once - it's *our* problem. (Communicate, use dialogue, ask for what you need.)
    2. Abuse me twice - it's *my* problem. (Block aggression, assert, and protect your rights.)
    3. Try it a third time - *I'm out of here.* (Put space between you and the abuser.)
- Don't wait for the Dragon or the system that supports a dysfunctional environment to change.
- Don't procrastinate.
- ***Act.***

Disarm Dragons with Assertive Steps

- *Sidesteps*
- *Turnarounds*
- *Fire Extinguishers*

Try these ideas for communication as you track your Dragon, deal effectively with the six signature patterns (Chapter 3), and remain free and unintimidated by Dragon's power games.
(See Chapters 4, 8, 9, 10, and 11.)

Try a Sidestep or a Fire Extinguisher for Deception

These techniques work as follows: you spot the classic deceptive practices of the Dragon in your workplace, and both you and the boss know about a dishonest situation. You are aware that you are vulnerable for being set up as a scapegoat unless you intervene. However, you are reluctant to be a whistle-blower since the Dragon has the power, and others are not yet aware of the dishonesty. To do nothing would send the message that you are willing to be a Doorkeeper for the boss's dishonest behavior.

Sidestep a direct accusation but ask the Dragon a question in private. Phrase your question to present the contradictions that you are seeing in the Dragon's behavior, then address your own ethical issue. For example:

> "How can I rationalize the summary report I heard you give in today's meeting in light of the quarterly report I submitted to you? The two reports are diametrically opposed, and you have left out some very important facts that the company needs to know. How can I justify my silence on these issues?"

If pressed further explain:

> "What I heard seemed to misrepresent the facts as we both know them. It poses an ethical question for me, since knowing the facts creates a strain on our working relationship, and once lost, trust is difficult to regain."

A direct statement leveling with the Dragon about your relationship says quite clearly, "I'm not willing to be Dragon food."

Whistle-blowers have a history of being fast food for the Dragons. If you took that course, you would be out of work immediately. What you need is time for the Dragon's deception to be discovered by others; meanwhile, gather support for your ethical position. If nothing happens as a result of your *sidestepping* move, repeat the same move in public at the next department meeting and add, "Could you help us understand the inconsistencies between the written report and the verbal one we heard at the last meeting?" Then watch the performance as the Dragon unloads a series of power games for the benefit of the audience.

Assess the responses to discover how many Doorkeepers there are to contend with and how much support the Dragon has. You may want to clean out your desk and be ready to move on with your life or you may find this organization to be worthy of your allegiance. Whatever happens, the experience should be enlightening.

If the issue is serious, one that might place you in danger of criminal indictment, you need a stronger *fire extinguisher* to disengage yourself from a possible setup. For example:

> "I can see that our interpretations of the facts are diametrically opposed, and I am unwilling to proceed without outside consultation. As I see it, the legal staff and the CEO need the missing information to make crucial decisions for the company's future. Will you be joining me in the conference or shall I proceed alone?"

Turnarounds - An Idea for Relationship Problems

(See Chapter 3, Signature Pattern No. 2., Relationships.)

This technique works as follows: your Dragon begins a classic divide-and-conquer game with gossip (See Chapter 4, Game No. 2.), which usually ends with the Dragon in control and the victim confused. However, you are wise to the power game and recognize the verbal overtures.

Dragon: "Just between you and me, I heard something Phil said about you that you need to know . . . and if you ever tell anyone I told you, I'll say you lied, but . . ."

You need a quick exit. You need to cut 'em off at the pass without exposing yourself to victimization. Try a *turn-around*.

You: "I'm as interested in juicy information as anyone, but I would feel uncomfortable with it unless Phil were here too. Thanks for letting me know. I'll make it a point to talk with him."

Turnarounds are typically compound sentences having a soft introductory clause followed by an assertive confrontation. Dragons have difficulty with honest, open communication and often use a rather rigid repertoire of power games. Therefore, Dragons expect a fairly structured response. When intended victims fail to respond according to expectations, Dragons are often confused and feel out of control and silenced.

In this example, the Dragon is thrown off balance by the unexpected response. Having identified you as a potential victim, the abuser is not expecting you to admit enjoying *juicy* information, nor are you expected to communicate directly with the second victim, Phil. Since you "thanked" the abuser for the information, the Dragon is left confused and speechless – disarmed for the time being.

Assessment - The Test:
When You Recognize the Test, Be Ready with a Fire Extinguisher Before Things Get Too Hot

(See Chapter 3, Signature Pattern No. 3, Assessment.)

Anyone who can recall having been "tested" for victimization in the past is keenly alert to the classic Dragon-testing situation. It's the novice worker who is often taken in by the move. Basically, it is when the boss or Doorkeeper becomes too intimate, "trusts" you with shocking or exciting "inside information," or tantalizes you with promises of great reward for supporting questionable or borderline business or personal practices while expecting your approval, silence, and capitulation.

You need to be ready to disarm the situation. This does not mean that you become a snitch or mount a white horse and come riding onto the scene as a hero. It means that you take care of yourself. Listen to your feelings, trust your ethical values, and guard your beliefs. You may be involved in the first stages of grooming for victimization, and there will be opportunities to extract yourself as long as you are alert and aware of having been tested.

This is the time for defensive action. "Hear no evil, see no evil, speak no evil," is one of the best courses. Even a Dragon has trouble intimidating a victim who refuses to cooperate by taking the bait. Find a legitimate reason to put distance between yourself and your boss. A restroom break is always acceptable to give you time to think. For example:

During an out-of-state conference, your Dragon suggests going into a questionable neighborhood for drugs, but you do not want to be involved in illegal antics. You don't want to offend the group, but you don't want to be a victim either. Try an assertive fire extinguisher before things get too hot. Simply state what it is that you are willing to do and then do it.

> "I'm willing to share a cab with you, but I am not interested in the Sucker's Den, so I'll be getting out at the Family Inn. I'll see you in the morning. I'm getting a good night's sleep before the big presentation in the morning."

If the testing includes alcohol and drugs and you cannot leave the scene immediately, fill your glass with water and join the group while staying alert for an exit but put distance between yourself and the activity in which they want you to be involved.

Disarm Grooming with a Silent Fire Extinguisher

(See Chapter 3, Signature Pattern No. 4, Grooming.)

Grooming always involves training the victim to disregard the instinctive anger alarm in favor of promised rewards, flattering remarks, favors, or other bait. Victims may find themselves subjected to verbal abuses, physical abuses, or perverse sexual overtures in private when there are no witnesses and it is their word against the Dragon's power. A video camera in your office or a small tape recorder with you at all times (even if it is off) can discourage unwanted private overtures and serve as an unspoken fire extinguisher. However, be direct and open about what you're doing when asked. "Yes, that is a camera. It's for my protection just in case I ever need it."

If a Silent Fire Extinguisher Does Not Work, Try a Loud One

Stay alert to your anger and guard against excusing the Dragon's intimidating words or behavior. One of the best methods of disarming is a loud assertive statement that registers disbelief. For example: "Mr. Zebra! I can't believe that you would risk your career at XYZ Industries for a grope!" If you need something stronger try, "I'm shocked, but I believe in straight talk. I never mix business and pleasure. Let's make sure it never happens again."

Ostracizing Always Requires Turnarounds in Question Form

(See Chapter 3, Signature Pattern No. 5, Ostracizing.)

If people seem to be avoiding you or a coworker has stopped talking to you and you are puzzled by a sudden change in your social status, you need to question those involved. Begin by asking yourself, "Have I said or done anything to offend or hurt others in my workplace?" If you can honestly say "no," then ask the same question of coworkers who are involved in your feelings of estrangement. You might say,

> "When the group goes to lunch or when there is a break, lately I've been feeling left out of the loop, and I'm wondering if there is something wrong. Could it be that I've said something that offended someone or done something insensitive that may have hurt someone's feelings? Or perhaps I'm being too sensitive myself. Can you give me some feedback?"

It is best to pose your questions to coworkers individually and in private. If your boss is a Dragon and is using the divide-and-conquer ploy, they may be in the process of being victimized too. Your coworkers, unaware of being set up for a power play, may fear courting disfavor from the boss by talking to you in public.

You might want to continue by asking, "Is there something I need to know that others aren't saying directly to me that could explain my feelings of being shunned?"

If you still have no answers, you might hypothesize that this issue is between you and the coworker and follow up with:

> Apparently you and I need to talk. What do we need to do to be more comfortable with each other? I miss the times when we could talk and work together without walking on eggshells. I'm willing to do anything within my power to understand and make things better between us.

Your next move might be to address the boss with a turnaround, a thinly veiled confrontation in an open question form designed to disclose your feelings and open a dialogue in order to turn around a difficult situation. For example: "Have you ever been in a position where you felt demeaned, excluded from the group, and puzzled about the reasons why?"

If the boss isn't a Dragon, you may initiate a very important breakthrough conversation and get directions that will provide insight and help you make changes for the better. True Dragons, however, typically respond with power plays - since you have "stepped on the Dragon's tail" by voicing your feelings and concerns. Thoroughly groomed victims don't approach Dragons, so your veiled confrontation can confuse and disarm the Dragon, providing temporary relief for you.

Be alert. Don't expect lasting changes but do be prepared for a Doorkeeper in your future if your boss is a Dragon. Conversely, be ready to make personal changes if the boss is not a Dragon and the problem is within your domain.

Numbing And Nullifying

(See Chapter 3, Signature Pattern No. 6, Numbing.)

Perhaps the most devastating process a victim undergoes in the toxic atmosphere of a dysfunctional workplace is the numbing of personal feelings, values, and ethics. When fear replaces righteous indignation and beliefs become undermined, workers no longer question corrupt practices or abuses; they join the dysfunctional culture. They may become automatons with little concern for the plight of other abused workers, the company, or its customers. With their emotions numbed, workers become Dragon food to be toyed with, abused, chewed up, preserved for further snacking, or devoured – a very precarious position indeed. Those who are treated as Dragon food are typically in denial. They believe that victimizing others is part of the job that workers must put up with unless they want to be fired.

If you no longer question practices that you would actively resist in any other setting, then it is time to take a reality check. Study the following Dragon-proofing table to find out whether you may have been brainwashed and are now numb and in denial or whether you are developing good Dragon-proofing skills to offset your Dragon's influence.

The first column, Brainwashing and Grooming Process, represents the Dragon fire and smoke present in the workplace.

Dragon Fire: Lists typical abusive activities of Dragons in the workplace.

Dragon Smoke: Presents those thoughts and feelings that the Dragon wants you to believe and feel as a result of being controlled and victimized.

The second column, Resistance and Recovery, sketches the the Dragon-taming and Dragon-proofing skills used by intended victims who are unwilling to become Dragon food.

Dragon-Taming: Lists many of the breakthroughs that targeted victims have as they gain awareness and study Dragon tracking and the power games that Dragons play.

Dragon-Proofing: Presents basic beliefs, thoughts, and deliberate activities designed to create resistance to victimization.

If the first column describes your experience with your boss and your current thoughts, you are most likely being brainwashed. If the second column is more representative of your awareness and current thinking processes, you are developing skills in Dragon-taming while Dragon-proofing yourself.

Disarming Dragons: Table 13-1

Brainwashing and Grooming Process *(Dragon Fire / Dragon Smoke)*	**Resistance and Recovery Process** *(Dragon-Taming / Dragon-Proofing)*
Dragon uses subtle negative comments / Victim is unaware of the Dragon's techniques	Victim understands anger alarm / Believes in his or her competency as a worker

Brainwashing and Grooming Process *(Dragon Fire / Dragon Smoke)*	**Resistance and Recovery Process** *(Dragon-Taming / Dragon-Proofing)*
Dragon isolates victim / Victim feels hurt and betrayed	***Victim spots Dragon tracks / Seeks support from family, friends, and other isolates***
Negative comments increase in frequency / Victim is confused and pulls away, blames "stress"	Victim understands Dragon behavior; alert and expecting games / Takes care of self physically and mentally
Dragon begins nit-picking, filing reprimands/Victim is stressed and feels stuck, angry, and scared	***Victim requests clarifications, expectations, and complaints in writing; documents everything / Increases positive stress***
Dragon alerts Doorkeeper; criticism increases / Victim immobilized; efficiency decreases	Alert to Dragon-tracking; does not respond as a victim / Reviews signature patterns
Dragon reports "failures" to superiors / Victim tries harder; errors increase	***Victim is prepared; does not respond emotionally / Knows rights, takes action, and makes decisions***
Dragon threatens victim / Victim is shocked, scared, confused; depression increasing	Recognizes tactics; documents all contacts; surveys options / Thinks rationally; recognizes freedom to make choices

Brainwashing and Grooming Process *(Dragon Fire / Dragon Smoke)*	Resistance and Recovery Process *(Dragon-Taming / Dragon-Proofing)*
Threats and pressures increase / Victim blames stress or illness; immobilized by fear	***Victim does homework; seeks legal and career consultation / Makes requests; decides whether to stay or go***
Victim is transferred or fired / Feels distressed, trapped, and defeated; may seek inappropriate releases (drugs, affairs, etc.)	Politely refuses offer for transfer or resignation; makes counter offers in lieu of legal actions / Tells the truth; faces reality
The Dragon is in control/ Victim feels third-degree anger, is very depressed, and withdraws completely	***Victim has alternative plans; knows options /True to beliefs and ethics; can handle and cope with uncertain future***

No matter where they exist, Dragons can be disarmed and tamed by your being resistant to denial and numbing and by using the five steps presented in this book. The next chapter of your life is up to you. Take charge! Make your choices with courage and determination based on the new information that you have gained and careful consideration of the many options that you have.

Now you can say: "My boss is (or is not) a Dragon! I'm not willing to be Dragon food. Furthermore, now I can do something about it!" Act now and take control of your future.

Epilogue

A Word to the Organization

Family therapy has articulated the role of the abuser in the home and has presented a clear picture of the pathological persecutor/victim relationship. Often abuse patterns are hidden for generations by ignorance, guilt, and denial; it is considered something that *just happens*. Society has become more aware of abusive actions and the resulting long-term devastation that can occur to the family unit as well as its members. But what industry and other organizations do not understand is that the same abusive tactics are often carried out in the workplace under the guise of *good management*. Employee abuse is ignored, misunderstood, and thought of as inevitable. As a result, acts of workplace violence are viewed as random or something that *just happens* as a result of a few disgruntled employees.

It is now time to look around, wise up, and drop the assumption that when there is unexplained agitation or when the bottom line goes into negative numbers that it is simply a correction in the market place. Any organization could be experiencing the domino effects of a dysfunctional system complete with Dragons, Doorkeepers, and incredibly abusive practices. Abusive management might even be considered one of the major problems facing American business because none of the other problems can be solved as long as there are undetected Dragons silently feeding in the workplace.

Since the days of Levi Strauss in 1906, the Great Northern Railway in 1923, the labor movements of the 1930's, and the input of W. Edwards Deming and others since the 1940's, American business has slowly been evolving from a paternalistic /military / dominating management style to a more egalitarian "systems" model. Today's literature is replete with descriptions of the most successful organizations being those that have highly motivated and productive workers and creative leadership supported by multiple feedback loops. A free flow of information, uninhibited by abusive power and control, is the lifeblood of creativity and a necessary component of business dynamics in today's rapidly changing workplace. It is important that loyal employees feel respected, needed, and trusted. Staffs must believe that they will not be destroyed for making honest mistakes. They must be treated fairly and with respect for their knowledge, creative contributions to the organization, and their service to customers and to the community at large.

Egalitarian working conditions are uncomfortable for Dragons. Their signature patterns emerge and become quite obvious when enlightened managers begin to track them. There is no single symptom that stands out and screams, "The organization is in trouble; there's a Dragon in your midst!" It is, rather, a pattern of problems (some appearing to be totally unrelated in what railroad CEO Gilbert Gillette terms "the theory of seemingly unrelated events") that provides the initial warnings. Organizational goals and objectives get lost in the chaos of a dysfunctional system. For example:

> In a retaliation power play, one railroad bully laid off several essential switch crews and labeled it a cost-reduction move in his report to the CEO. As a result, a large meat packing company's delivery deadlines were not met and product safety was compromised. The company suffered a huge loss in the form of spoiled meat. The railroad CEO wondered why this former customer began to ship by truck at an increased shipping cost. He never noticed the rather obvious correlation between the two "unrelated events."

> The health department temporarily closed a well-known, upscale restaurant because of a sudden outbreak of food poisoning. A disgruntled former employee was blamed for the incident but never charged with a crime. The boss, known for his Dragon-like behavior toward employees and customers, wondered why business steadily declined. Former customers, preferring not to be victims, had no trouble sensing a wake-up call and simply took their business

elsewhere. As new employees became aware of working conditions, they too moved on to new jobs. Eventually, the establishment was put up for sale and several of the surviving employees moved on to open their own restaurant at another location.

A truck line laid off experienced mechanics who expressed serious concerns about their workloads. The remaining mechanics were unable to keep up with work expectations. The company accused workers of a deliberate slowdown then wondered why shippers switched to other truck lines when trucks were not available to pick up new loads.

Warning Signals for the CEO

Long before the bottom line delivers the message of bad news, astute corporate executives need to be aware of signals that are sounding a wake-up call for troubles ahead. They should look for the following early warning signs and investigate wherever they see problems or suspicious behavior.

1. A flurry of changes followed by a deliberate decrease in research support or funding
2. Down-sizing and budget cuts, which often begin with maintenance programs, that give short-term results but are destructive over the long run
3. A reported decrease in customer complaints that parallels decreased positive comments, as well as a general decrease in customer feedback
4. Increased loss, damage, and accident ratios that mirror increased rates of product return from customers

5. Job satisfaction surveys appear positive while in reality employee morale is low
6. Employee Assistance Program budget analysis indicates increased referrals for anger control, stress management, and depression
7. One or more incidents of employee rage unreported or discounted as random violence or mental disorder
8. Depression is evident, and a suicide or questionable death has taken place
9. There are biased employee files accompanied by obvious Rumplestiltskin ploys on the part of supervisors
10. Increased absenteeism, retirement, and resignation rates
11. Spontaneity and creative employee suggestions decrease
12. Employees "walk on eggshells" around certain managers
13. Sabotage, minor pilfering, slowdowns, and undercover resistance increase while supervisory reports remain positive
14. There are highly competitive power concentrations within management groups that employ very destructive "turf protection" tactics, Dragon games, and power plays
15. The signature patterns of Dragons and Doorkeepers are obvious when management takes time to compare reports with personal investigations
16. Rumors of unreported events involving discrimination

Dragons, like cockroaches, prefer the dark. When the spotlight of awareness is focused on their signature patterns and their abusive power games are exposed, Dragons run for cover. They survive in the darkness of ignorance. Without support, they leave.

Advice for the Therapist

Exposing Dragons to the light of awareness is extremely painful to them and can trigger outbursts that range from destroying physical objects to harming those whom they consider victims. In extreme cases, where the abuser is faced with the reality of inescapable personal loss, suicide can be an option, especially if the Dragon can destroy others in the process. While they seldom directly attack people of larger stature, some have been known to retaliate against completely innocent bystanders in a blind rage. Therapy with violent people is hazardous at best, and prognosis for significant change is poor.

Dragons are usually quite bright, but the majority can meet the criteria established by the American Psychiatric Association (APA) for personality disorders. They have an enduring pattern of perceiving and interpreting themselves, others, and events that deviates markedly from the norm. They seem to have insatiable appetites for admiration but an inability to feel empathy for others. They can manage social relationships on a superficial basis as long as they remain in absolute control. Those who believe that they are in love with a Dragon cannot hope to feel that love returned because Dragons are in love with themselves.

Clinically, these characteristics are considered evidence of a personality disorder. Some Dragons display only the Narcissistic features and others warrant the added designations of Borderline or Antisocial disorders in their diagnosis. The following descriptions and information can be found in the DSM-IV put out by the APA:

301.81 Narcissistic Personality Disorder

Typically they exhibit five or more of the following characteristics:

1. A grandiose sense of self-importance
2. A preoccupation with fantasies of unlimited success, power, brilliance, beauty, or ideal love
3. A belief that he or she is special or unique and can only be understood by other high-status people or institutions
4. An excessive need for admiration
5. Has a sense of entitlement, meaning unreasonable expectations of favorable treatment or automatic compliance with his or her expectations
6. Takes advantage of or exploits others
7. Lacks empathy, unwilling to recognize or identify with the feelings or needs of others
8. Is jealous of others or believes them to be envious of him or her
9. Displays arrogant, haughty behaviors or attitudes

301.83 Borderline Personality

1. Frantic efforts to avoid real or imagined abandonment
2. Unstable interpersonal relationships alternating between idealization and deviation
3. Impulsiveness

301.7 Antisocial Personality Disorder

1. Deceitfulness, repeated lying, conning others for personal profit or pleasure
2. Irritability and aggressiveness
3. Reckless disregard for safety of self or others

Though sometimes referred for anger therapy, Dragons typically don't enter treatment. If they do, they seldom return after the first session. Some therapists may find such patients to be very difficult and uncooperative.

Classic anger control and behavioral therapy, which have been found to be fairly effective with first- and second-degree anger problems, is seldom effective with Dragons' third-degree anger and their personality disorders. In *AMP Therapy: Strategies for Anger Management and Violence Prevention*, Winnifred Taylor discusses further information regarding high-impact techniques for anger therapy.

Abusers are generally too egocentric or grandiose to consider their behavior a problem to anyone else and yet too vulnerable to risk self-analysis. Dragons, passionately avoiding therapy, usually move on to infiltrate other organizations in a desperate drive to regain power. Unfortunately, this passion is often seen as appealing to the new organization looking for a leader and not realizing that they are interviewing a Dragon. Since Dragons seldom get therapy, therapists are typically called upon to treat their victims and families, those for whom the domino effect of long-term abusive treatment has left its scars.

Treating Victims

Clients who have been exposed to abuse typically show classic symptoms of depression and a moderate to high risk of physical deterioration or self-injury. Often, there are somatic complaints as well as actual physical injuries that require medical consultation. Denial is typically a problem, and it varies depending on the type of abuse, the setting, and the amount of time that the distress was endured. Where isolation and both physical and emotional control have been absolute, such as in kidnapping, prison camps, and dysfunctional families, victims often display learned helplessness and emotional attachment to their abusers. For example, battered children cling to the abusive parent's leg to avoid separation and blame themselves for misbehaving. Battered wives may return to their abusers and blame themselves for causing the problem.

Where absolute control is not possible, such as in the workplace, the systematic abuse leaves victims confused, socially isolated, self-blaming, and fearful. Such tactics deplete the victims' personal power and self-confidence. Thus we see learned helplessness along with distorted perceptions of the abuser's power in the clinical picture. Workers feel trapped by fears of reprisal, economic pressures, guilt, and self-blame. In our culture, males in particular have difficulty admitting powerlessness and helplessness. Where threat triggers autonomic fight-or-flight sensations but fear blocks expression of anger, denial often becomes a basic component of the therapeutic problem.

Confusion coupled with helplessness and depression makes it extremely difficult for victims to identify reality, let alone identify options and then take meaningful steps toward change. They may also require professional help for a number of *blind-alley* problems, such as budget bickering, infidelity, family stress, career counseling, alcohol abuse, and the like.

However, enlightened counselors and therapists who are acquainted with abuse issues are seldom sidetracked by such initial complaints. They recognize that dealing with third-degree anger issues coupled with depression and denial requires a multi-modal approach that often includes journaling and reality-based experiences combined with cognitive and affective therapy. With the exception of crisis situations, drug therapy alone is not the treatment of choice. Although working through depression is a painful process, it is also a learning process where the clients discover their unique personal resources and practice new coping skills.

With the support of the therapeutic process, clients move from confusion and helplessness to a place where both thoughts and feelings become clear. Options are clarified and understood; choices are made. As clients let go of the past and move on under their own personal power, they gain greater insight and a feeling of personal responsibility for improvement in both attitude and behavior.

When prescribed medications are too great a part of the therapy, clients tend to attribute their progress to the drugs. They seem to remain *helpless* for a longer period of time than those who proceed without receiving pharmaceuticals. For some people, learned dependency is often less threatening than making major changes, letting go, and moving on. Medication may provide another opportunity to deny their own responsibility for the changes that they make in therapy and thus prolong the process of working through tough issues and taking charge of their lives.

A Note to the EAP Counselor

Just as abusive parents claim that they are acting on behalf of their children, organizational Dragons often believe that what they are doing is sound management. Victims typically believe the same mythology and may never utter the word "abuse." With both the company and the victim in denial, the counselor must be alert to helpful treatment plans and referral networks.

In functional organizations with a single Dragon, the EAP Counselor may be the first to detect the abusive patterns. It is important to help victims become aware of their options and provide them with realistic decision-making skills. Just as in any counselor-client relationship, confidentiality has top priority. It is not the counselor's place to become a "Dragon killer," but it may well be within the role of the EAP counselor to provide education and training to management staff and employees about the problem of abuse in the workplace.

In dysfunctional organizations, it is important to remain non-judgmental. For example, it may be irresponsible to assume that the employees referred for "stress" are always bringing it on themselves and need to learn how to develop a thicker skin and get along better with the boss.

Like crisis counselors everywhere, EAP counselors need to be alert to the signs of abuse and victimization and be ready to prevent the escalation of violence or potential suicide, all while dealing with their regular caseloads each day.

Appendix I

A Postscript for the Reader

Since this book breaks new ground in understanding and dealing with the taboo subjects of power, control, and victimization in the workplace, you may want to use it as your personal study guide. As you become adept at dealing with your own issues, you may find others in similar circumstances seeking your support and advice. Reach out to others.

Idea: Set up your own weekly book discussion group of interested people for support while disarming the Dragons in your lives. Victimization typically leaves emotional scars that may last for years. Whether a person is currently under the influence of a Dragon, recovering from the results of abuse, preventing abusive practices within the workplace, or being impacted by the domino effects of an abusive situation, you now have some practical answers. For example:

1. A 14-week plan would include: one organizational meeting with a goal-setting agenda, twelve meetings covering one or more chapters per week devoted to discussions, and one closure meeting for evaluation, sharing, and future planning. A 7-week plan would include one organizational meeting, five meetings covering one *step* per meeting, and one closure meeting.
2. Be prepared to answer, discuss, and implement all exercises and questions that the group chooses to discuss at each meeting.
3. Although group members should be encouraged to keep their own diaries, such personal documents should not be shared in the group.

Using This Book as a Study Guide

The book is arranged in chronological order and can easily serve as a study guide for one reader or small discussion groups as follows:

Week 1

Step I: Recognize the Mystification

Read Chapter 1	"Victimization by Mystification" How it's done in three sneaky stages
Read Chapter 2	"What You Need to Know About Getting Started" Document
Discuss:	Mystification: Notice how strong feelings combined with confusion are typically part of the process. Recognize how abusers use power and persuasion to mislead potential victims.
Discuss:	Victimizing Process: 1. Grooming 2. The Setup 3. The Hook
Activity:	Prepare a special spiral notebook for your personal Dragon diary (DD) for future use in documenting feelings and experiences. Answer the questions at the end of the chapter and add the most relevant concepts to your DD notebook.

Week 2

Step II: Unmask The Dragon

Read Chapter 3	"Dragon Tracking "
Discuss:	The six signature patterns of Dragons: D-R-A-G-O-N Pay attention to the various roles of Dragons, Doorkeepers, Doormats, and victims and the testing process used to select candidates for victimization.
Activity:	Complete the Dragon-Tracking Checklist 3-1.

Week 3

Read Chapter 4	"Power Games Dragons Play" 1. Blind Man's Bluff 2. Divide and Conquer 3. Heads I Win. Tails You Lose 4. Musical Chairs 5. Blame and Shame, That's Our Game 6. Rumpelstiltskin Ploy
Discuss:	The six common power games Dragons play Summary and Exercises.
Activity:	Complete the Game Spotting Checklist 4-2.

Week 4

Step III: Honor Your Anger

Read Chapter 5	"Trust Your Anger Alarm" First-, second-, and third-degree anger

Discuss: Six anger traps and eight escapes.

Activity: Discuss Summary and answer Questions.

Week 5

Read Chapter 6 "Deal with Depression"
Pay attention to the nine feelings typically reported by angry, stressed people.

Discuss: Self Study Checklist 6-1, Anger/Depression Checklist 6-2, Depressive Symptom Checklist 6-3.

Activity: Contrast the list of quotes on pages 83-84 with the last question in Chapter 6, page 89.

Week 6

Read Chapter 7 "Handling Stress"
Pay attention to each of the suggestions including: understanding, attitude pacing, variety, relaxing, self-talk, exercise, nutrition, and other suggestions for dealing with feelings.

Discuss: Personal experiences and successful methods for handling distress.

Activity: Complete Step III Summary and Questions.

Week 7

Step IV: Disarm the Dragons

Read Chapter 8 "Hang on to Your Beliefs"
Pay attention to Dragon-taming and Dragon-proofing skills.

Discuss:	Personal experiences and successful Dragon-taming and Dragon-proofing skills.
Activity:	Read Summary and share answers to the review questions.

Week 8

Read Chapter 9	"Dragon Fire Extinguishers"
	Pay attention to extinguishers for toxic pressures, gang-ups, belittling, and non-questions.
Discuss:	Summary and Dragon fire extinguishers.
Activity:	Fill in Practice Disarming Dragons Table 9-2 with your own experiences in: 1. Brainwashing, by recognizing Dragon tracks 2. Grooming, by recognizing Dragon smoke 3. Resisting, by Dragon-taming thoughts 4. Recovering, by Dragon-proofing yourself

Week 9

Read Chapter 10	"Subtle Abuse "
	Pay attention to methods of detecting and disarming subtle patterns of abusive discrimination.
Discuss:	Discrimination Isolation Economic Abuses Workload Abuses
Activity:	Beginning with the Dragon smoke, Dragon-taming, and Dragon-proofing thoughts,

choose one example of subtle abuse and list ideas on how to disarm Dragons.

Week 10

Read Chapter 11 "Deliberate Abuse"

Pay attention to harassment, the Rumplestiltskin ploy, and the other torments, including several versions of transfers, etc.

Discuss: Summary

Activity: Share examples of your personal experiences with deliberate abuses and discuss Dragon-proofing ideas.

Week 11

Step V: Take Action

Read Chapter 12 "Look at All the Options"

Discuss: All options but focus on the fifteen ideas most relevant to the you or your group's situation(s).

Activity: There are six exercises in this chapter. Complete as many as you wish, using your DD to record your thoughts.

Week 12

Read Chapter 13 "Do It!"

Focus on the following concepts:

Overcoming procrastination
Discerning fear from caution
Considering all options
Making choices
Disarming Dragons

Discuss: All ideas and suggestions, paying particular attention to Disarming Dragons Table 13-1 (page 215) and assessing your progress in developing good Dragon-proofing skills to offset the Dragon's negative influence.

Activity: Role-play situations from your own notebook and develop your own creative ideas for disarming aggressive actions aimed in your direction.

Week 13

Epilogue: A Word to the Organization
Advice for the Therapist
A Note to the EAP Counselor

Review: Steps I, II, III, IV, and V

Discuss: How does information about abusive practices in the workplace impact busy organizations as well as workers and their families?

Activity: After reviewing all five steps leading to freedom from workplace abuse, choose one step that you feel is important to you or your group. Return to that step and share (and/or note in your diary) your own experiences or insights gathered from your reading.

Week 14

Closure Having reviewed all five steps in the book and your own Dragon diary, share with others (or write in your DD) the most useful concepts that you have gathered from your study of this book. What conclusions have you drawn about your boss, about your career, and about yourself? What changes have you made? What are your plans?

Appendix II

Comparative Abuse

The behavior of Dragon bosses correlates very closely with the research done by Albert D. Biderman regarding the behavior of prisoner of war (POW) camp guards. Biderman created a chart of coercion in *Report on Torture,* which was published by Amnesty International.

The chart has been used by several writers in books on domestic violence, such as *Rape in Marriage* by Diana H. Russell, illustrating how domestic abuse is similar to that of the POW guards. A correlation can also be drawn between abuse in three different environments: the POW camp, the domestic environment, and the workplace. Abusers from each of these areas use the same techniques for similar reasons and with similar effects. These abusers use methods such as:

- Isolation
- Monopolization of perception
- Induced debility; exhaustion
- Threats
- Occasional indulgences
- Demonstration of omnipotence
- Degradation
- Enforcement of trivial demands

In each arena, *isolation* serves the same purpose. It cuts off the victim, spouse, or prisoner from any social support and thereby lessens any ability to resist. The victims have no one to rely upon and have no one with whom to share concerns or emotions. In each case, the victim becomes totally dependent on the abuser.

In environments that are completely controlled by the abuser, victims attach all of their attention on this person and become fixated with complying with demands. The abusers are able to gain complete *monopolization of perception.* The abuser is the victim's only source for information in each arena and often gives false data to keep the victim under control. This eliminates any stimuli that competes with those controlled by the abuser.

In the three environments, abuse is sustained over an extended period of time. In the domestic situation and the POW camp, there is a greater likelihood that physical abuse will occur. Emotional and mental assaults are guaranteed in all three. Physical and emotional abuse tactics cause *induced debility* and *exhaustion*. The victim's physical energies and stamina become depleted, and the victim is left emotionally drained. In POW camps, prisoners' physical ability to resist is weakened. Victims in all three arenas suffer damaged health.

Threats are a commonality amongst all abusers. Threats cultivate anxiety and despair; they create fear and through it immobilization. In the workplace, threats include firing, demotions, and false accusations. In the home, threats include murder, suicide, or kidnapping of children. The POW guard may threaten deprivation, torture, or death.

Offering *occasional indulgences* is another technique the three types of abusers share. The abuser provides a short respite from assaults in order to keep the victim functioning or living enough to comply with future demands and abuse. In the office, the Dragon may act nice for a short time or simply leave the victim alone. In the domestic setting, the abuser may apologize for violence and "makeup" with the victim. A guard may give a starving prisoner a little bread. These indulgences provide positive motivation for compliance with future abuse.

All of these abusers attempt to make a *demonstration of omnipotence.* They want to show their victims the futility of resistance. Dragons and domestic abusers continually tell their victims that no one would ever believe their stories if they told nor would anyone offer assistance. A guard impresses on prisoners the fact that their lives are in his or her hands. A guard controls every aspect of a prisoner's life: food, environment, schedule, and execution.

Another technique of these abusers is the use of *degradation.* Abusers degrade victims both publicly and privately. In the workplace, Dragons put their victims in humiliating and degrading situations until the victims give up resistance, keep silent, and support the abuser. Suffering from such degradation, the victim may become abusive to others in the workplace or at home. This process is similar within the domestic environment. The abuser places the spouse in humiliating and degrading situations, and here as well, the spouse may become abusive to the children or others. In the POW camps, degradation reduces the prisoner to "animal level" concerns. Degradation makes the cost of resisting appear more damaging than capitulation.

These abusers also use *enforcement of trivial demands* in order to control victims. In each environment, the abusers control every minute of the victims' time and actions. In the home, the abuser says, "You have 30 minutes to go to the store and get back here." In the workplace, the boss may call random meetings or assign so much work that much of it must be done at home. The tactic creates a habit of compliance in the victims.

Abusers in each of the three environments share tactics of abuse, which often create similar results for the victims. The methods are comparable as are the effects and purposes. These examples demonstrate how abuse parallels itself across a range of situations and experiences.

Bibliography

American Psychiatric Association. Diagnostic and Statistical Manual of Mental Disorders. Fourth Edition, Text Revision, DSM-IV-TR. Washington, DC: American Psychiatric Association, 2000.

Biderman, Albert. Report on Torture. New York: Amnesty International, 1975.

Bing, Stanley. Crazy Bosses. New York: William Morrow & Company, 1992.

Dorin, Patrick. "Can Site-Based Management Systems Benefit the Transportation Industry?" *Journal of Transportation Law, Logistics and Policy* (Winter, 1996): 207.

"The Critical Need for Inter-Departmental / Cultural Understanding and Teamwork Between Marketing and Operations in the Transportation Industry," *Journal of Transportation Law, Logistics and Policy* (Winter 1995): 153.

Frances, Allen, Michael B. First, Harold Alan Pincus, and Thomas A. Widiger. Diagnostic Criteria From DSM-IV. Washington, DC: The American Psychiatric Association, 1995.

Loehr, James. Stress For Success. New York: Random House, 1997.

Mahoney, David and Richard Restak. The Longevity Strategy. New York: John Wiley, 1998.

Selye, Hans. The Stress of Life. New York: McGraw-Hill Book Company, 1958.

Taylor, John F. Is It Fear or Procrastination? Salem, Oregon: FACT'R, 1998.

Taylor, Winnifred J. AMP Therapy: Strategies For Anger Management And Violence Prevention. Salem, Oregon: Excelsior Books,1995.

Glossary

Doorkeeper:	A person who is willing to accept and dole out abuse and protect the Dragon's interests in exchange for temporary favorable treatment from a Dragon.
Doormat:	A victim willing to remain in an abusive system.
Dragon:	An abuser, an extremely self-serving individual with Narcissistic traits coupled with an ability to smooth talk others into their schemes. The Dragon is able to use the *lie* to accomplish almost anything.
Dragon Breath:	Negativity, insults, lies, verbal abuse, and nonverbal abuse aimed toward targeted victims.
Dragon Fire:	Animated or provocative verbal or physical attacks designed to terrorize, victimize, control, and exploit people.
Dragon-Proofing:	The process of getting in touch with one's own basic belief system, including ethics and moral judgments as an antidote to future victimization.
Dragon Smoke:	Deliberate lies and manipulative moves intended to cloud a victim's thinking or mystify the working environment, including misinformation and half-truths.

Dragon-Taming:	Rational replacement thoughts to counter the Dragon fire and smoke, to free victims' thinking processes, and to counter the negative impact of the Dragon's influence.
Dragon Tracks:	Specific, identifiable signature patterns, games, and ploys – signs that point out a Dragon and demonstrate that a Dragon has been at work.

About the Authors

Winnifred Taylor, Ph.D. formulated many of the psychological concepts of this book based on her extensive research into anger, violence, and victimization. She is the author of the book and audio tape series, *Anger Answers*. As Professor Emeritus at the University of Wisconsin-Superior, she is known for her expertise in teaching new concepts and multimodal insight skills in counseling and psychology to professionals.

Patrick C. Dorin, Ph.D. is currently an assistant principal for a Wisconsin high school. He has many years of management experience and has been an instructor at the university level for more than 20 years. He has written many articles and several books on management and the railroading industry.

John Taylor, Ph.D. is regarded as an innovative, forward-thinking trendsetter whose books, audio tapes, video productions, and seminars reflect insights from his thirty years of practice as a clinical psychologist. He is president of A.D.D.-Plus, Training and Resources for Attention Disorder and Related Conditions. Among his many published works are *From Defiance to Cooperation, Anger Control Training*, and *Person to Person Awareness Techniques*. His publications and seminars are described in detail on the web at www.ADD-PLUS.com.